Global Training and Development

Michel Syrett and Jean Lammiman

- Fast-track route to supporting global company strategies through management development initiatives

- Covers the key areas of linking HR policy to global goals, designing and delivering management development initiatives across international boundaries, overcoming cultural differences and creating common aims and aspirations

- Examples and lessons from some of the world's leading companies, including the Disney Corporation, GlaxoSmithKline, Diageo, Volkswagen, General Electric, L'Oreal, BMW and Standard Chartered Bank, and ideas from some of the world's smartest thinkers including Michael Porter, Gary Hamel, Michael Eisner, Jack Welch, and Geert Hofstede

  Includes a glossary of key concepts and a comprehensive resources guide

First Published 2003 by
Capstone Publishing Limited (a Wiley company)
8 Newtec Place
Magdalen Road
Oxford OX4 1RE
United Kingdom
http://www.capstoneideas.com

CIP catalogue records for this book are available from the British Library and the US Library of Congress

ISBN 1-84112-443-5

Wiley also publishes its books in a variety of electronic formats. Some content that appears in print may not be available in electronic books.

Websites often change their contents and addresses; details of sites listed in this book were accurate at the time of writing, but may change.

Contents

Introduction to ExpressExec

ExpressExec is a completely up-to-date resource of current business practice, accessible in a number of ways – anytime, anyplace, anywhere. ExpressExec combines best practice cases, key ideas, action points, glossaries, further reading, and resources.

Each module contains 10 individual titles that cover all the key aspects of global business practice. Written by leading experts in their field, the knowledge imparted provides executives with the tools and skills to increase their personal and business effectiveness, benefiting both employee and employer.

ExpressExec is available in a number of formats:

» **Print** – 120 titles available through retailers or printed on demand using any combination of the 1200 chapters available.
» **E-Books** – e-books can be individually downloaded from ExpressExec.com or online retailers onto PCs, handheld computers, and e-readers.
» **Online** – http://www.expressexec.wiley.com/ provides fully searchable access to the complete ExpressExec resource via the Internet – a cost-effective online tool to increase business expertise across a whole organization.

» **ExpressExec Performance Support Solution (EEPSS)** – a software solution that integrates ExpressExec content with interactive tools to provide organizations with a complete internal management development solution.

» **ExpressExec Rights and Syndication** – ExpressExec content can be licensed for translation or display within intranets or on Internet sites.

To find out more visit www.ExpressExec.com or contact elound@wiley-capstone.co.uk.

Introduction

Every generation has its celebrity business captains and their observations, usually outlined in best-selling autobiographies published once they have stepped down from the top job, reflect the attitudes and obsessions of the age. Today it is Jack Welch, former chief executive of General Electric (GE), who expanded his corporation's markets into parts of the world that previously seemed impenetrable. A decade ago it was John Harvey-Jones, whose turnaround of the chemical giant ICI was largely internal and domestically centered.

DO WE, DON'T WE, WANT TO GO TO THE DANCE?

In his valedictory tome *Making it Happen: Reflections on leadership*, Harvey-Jones has a chapter "Do we want to be international?" – as if top 500 companies have a choice. While he comes across as a committed internationalist, whose formative years were spent in India as a child and in the navy commanding a ship crewed entirely by Germans, his reflections on cross-cultural skills were almost entirely personal.

Jack Welch would not have given the question "Do we want to be international?" a moment's hesitation. His attitude is "be global or die." His version of *Making it Happen*, the brashly titled *Jack: Straight from the gut*, makes this very clear. His frequently quoted adage, that if you do not control your destiny someone else will, was made in the context of his decision to aggressively expand into the European markets dominated by Osram and Philips before they aggressively expanded into his.

The debate in the last decade has been not *whether* to be global but *how*. And since, as this guide will stress, a company's global strategy reflects how it has tended to expand at home, different traditions and strategies have been pursued side by side. Welch's US strategy was to buy up ailing competitors and turn them around – and he saw no reason to water this strategy down to pander to cross-cultural sensitivities, once he turned his eye to broader horizons. His takeover and overhaul of the Hungarian light bulb manufacturer Tungsram, described in greater detail in Chapter 4 of this book, was a faithful execution of the dictum developed at Crotonville in the previous decade that each GE business had to be No. 1 or No. 2 in its markets, and if not they had to be "fixed, closed, or sold."

Foreign traditions meant nothing to him. He did not see people in the companies he took over in Europe as English, Italian, Swedish, Hungarian, or Russian. He saw them as valued GE employees in a "boundaryless" organization that knew no borders or constraints, whether these were internal or geographical. The accusation leveled at his company by Hungarian trade unions, lobby groups, and government officials that his methods were "American" and "alien" mystified and affronted both him and the then chief executive officer of the European Lighting Division, Chuck Pieper. The methods, in their eyes, were those of a company, not a country. Nationality was irrelevant.

But other companies have sought to grow by alliance and joint venture, not merger and acquisition. The national airlines of Europe, for example, have little remit to expand internationally for the sake of doing so, but rather as a means to protect and sustain their markets. The alliances they formed in the late 1990s, like the Star Alliance described in Chapter 6, do not have the aim to create a Welchian melting pot of cultures but to preserve and exchange the distinctive contributions of each company (and culture) for the good of the whole. The comment by Lufthansa's human resources (HR) director, Thomas Sattelberger, that he is a loyal member of both Lufthansa and the Star Alliance in the same way as he is simultaneously a Bavarian, a German, and a European perfectly reflects the rationale behind the HR strategy that binds the partners in the alliance together.

Regardless of the rationales and the strategies they underpin, and regardless of the reasons why companies choose to "go global," training and development are the only way that companies can achieve the synergies they want. As has been pointed out by Dave Ulrich, global HR champion and guru profiled in Chapter 8, exchanging information and creating new knowledge are the only means for organizations to achieve the magic formula of thinking globally but acting locally.

There is sometimes an unjustified glamor attached to global training. The mechanics of design and delivery are the same, whether the task is to create a consensus and exchange between employees in different buildings in the same town, in different towns in the same country, or in different corporate centers in a global network. In the age of the psychological and moral contract, modern training and development are as much about influencing how people think, see, and feel as determining what they do. This is as true of someone based in Baltimore as it is of someone based in Beijing.

But the contrasts lurking below the surface are that much more subtle and deeply rooted once national or regional borders are crossed. As Harvey-Jones concludes, ''The mere fact that one stays in the same sort of hotel almost anywhere in the world, that one drives the same sort of car, that it is now possible to communicate or e-mail from almost anywhere in the world, all give a superficial feeling of sameness. A sameness which is desperately misleading, and which must never be taken for granted.''

As good a starting point as any for this guide.

FURTHER READING

Harvey-Jones, J. (1988) *Making it Happen: Reflections on leadership*. HarperCollins, London.

Welch, J.F. (2001) *Jack: Straight from the gut*. Warner Books, New York.

Definition of Terms

Globalism has been defined in many ways, but the phrase that seems to stick is that international companies need to "think global, act local."

Unilever, for instance, became successful marketing laundry soaps in India only after it spent time studying the country's washing habits. Many people in India wash their laundry in rivers, on rocks or washboards. Unilever's boxed powder, which it had successfully marketed to the developed world for decades, doesn't work in these conditions. Also it is too expensive for local people. So the company changed the form of the soap from powder to small bricks, and then sold them for a few rupees each.

A SOAP BY ANY OTHER NAME

Sounds simple, doesn't it? But the thinking that led Unilever to make the change is more complex. The Unilever brand had to be kept intact. The quality of the soap had to remain high – look what happened to Nestlé's reputation in the wake of its selling low-grade baby milk in developing countries. At the same time, the manufacturing processes had to be flexible enough to allow for the making of small bricks (in manufacturing terms more costly to produce than soap powder in large boxes) at a unit price local people could afford.

Given that this required a significant shift in the company's well-established factory technology, senior executives (thinking globally) had to decide whether making soap bricks for Indian consumers (and therefore acting locally) was worth the effort. The sheer size of the market in India prompted them to think that it was. It might have been different if the country had been smaller and the new manufacturing processes less transferable to other developing countries.

In training terms, the implications of a "think global, act local" strategy are also more complex than you might think. Unilever needed local people on the ground who were able to spot the market opportunity that would be opened up by the change from powder in boxes to bricks. They needed to have an understanding of the company as a whole, and the right personal networks and lines of accountability to get the change accepted.

Local people with the right training were also needed to market and distribute the new format soap in communities that lacked conventional retail infrastructures. All of this needed to be underpinned by a corporate culture that fostered shared learning and the creation of new knowledge. A local manager may have spotted the opportunity but is he or she (and all the other people that are going to be involved inside the company) going to feel it is worth the effort of championing the change?

YOU SAY TOMATO...

The training and development challenges are therefore immense. The processes and supporting technology may be no different from what the company has carried out for decades, when its ambitions were less international, but the scope and scale will require the HR specialists on the ground to engage in their own "think global, act local" mindset.

In the days when international companies used cheap local labor to manufacture products designed by and for people in other countries, training was simply a matter of technology or knowledge transfer. Now, international companies have to train local people to help them design local products or deliver local services to local consumers in the same country or region that nonetheless meet international standards of excellence and help to build the company's international brand equity.

To acquire the skills, knowledge, and personal attributes to maintain this balance, these people will have to take part in a training program that is designed and run to international standards, and may entail them relocating either briefly or for longer periods of time. They may have been brought up in a culture that respects age and status, and yet work for a company where promotion is based purely on merit; a culture in which women or local people from other races are not socially mobile, when the company has a strict equal opportunities policy; or a culture where, until recently, your status as a manager or technical expert was predicated on your standing in the local communist, nationalist, religious, or other political party.

The company's international culture of "quality" and "boundary-lessness" may require them to work across different functions, when they have been used to working in jobs with tightly defined, specialist roles. It may require them to submit to regular 360-degree appraisal and feedback, when their authority in local firms has been unquestioned, least of all by subordinates. It may encourage them to share learning and ideas on a routine daily basis, when in local firms knowledge is power and therefore to be negotiated only for personal gain.

The assumptions made about the links (or lack of them) between business strategy and political policy may be radically different. A young American executive visiting prospective business contacts in Prague a few months after the Berlin Wall came down was astonished to be asked during a business party hosted by the family of a local plant manager: "Are you Americans going to betray us again?"

Subsequent questioning revealed that the man was referring to what people in Central Europe see as the sell-out of their countries by the West to Stalin at the Yalta Conference in 1945. To the questioner, an American business executive was representing not only the company he worked for but the government policy of his country as well – largely because under the political system from which the Czech Republic had recently emerged, the only managers allowed abroad on commercial business were members of the local communist party.

GROUND CONTROL TO...

The recognition that innovation, and the ability to foster it, is a competitive necessity has reinforced the challenge. Encouraging diversity is now not just a moral virtue but a commercial necessity. Michael Eisner, chief executive of the Disney Corporation, put it very well when he commented in an interview for *Harvard Business Review*:

"I'm not talking about diversity in skin color or ethnic background. I'm talking about diversity in point of view. We want people who work here to look at the world differently from each other. They can be white, they can be African-American, they can be Indian or Chinese or Latino – it doesn't really matter. The important thing is that they look at the same problem and bring their own individuality to the solution."

It is therefore not enough, as companies like Arthur Andersen and General Electric did, and still do, to ship recruits from around the world and drill them into providing consistent services to clients who are also global from any location in the world. If you want to "act local" as well as "think global," you need to preserve local identity and knowledge, and graft it onto the economies of scale and global brand equity achieved by the company.

This has been aided by two other HR-related forces that have transformed organizations in the last decade. The first is organizational learning. Ever at the front of these trends, big utility providers like BP and Shell have set up "learning and development" functions to augment their training and development activities. This is not simply an affectation. It emphasizes that the aim of all modern training initiatives – explored in more detail in the ExpressExec guide *Management Development* – is to capture and exploit the thinking of front-line workers every bit as much as it is to transfer skills or inculcate company values and missions.

The second force is e-learning. Whether it is delivered by a business school or the organization itself (see the Standard Chartered Bank and Shell cases, respectively, in Chapter 5), the capacity of intranets, discussion databases, or Web-based reference sites to cut across conventional barriers to learning at a distance have impacted on global training and development initiatives more than any other.

Taken together, the development of a diverse global workforce, the need to share learning and create new knowledge to meet global ambitions, and the capacity of electronic learning to make this happen have turned traditional training and development from a top-down to a bottom-up activity. As the University of Michigan's Dave Ulrich concludes:

> "Global success requires the capability of viewing the organization from both a space-shuttle and a ground-level perspective, consequently feeling a fervent sense of accountability for one's own plot of land.
>
> "When devising global HR policies, it is worth remembering that, despite the rhetoric, only a handful of people has truly global responsibilities. Nearly all executives, managers, supervisors and staff carry out activities at a much more local level. To work most effectively, they need to feel connected to the worldwide organization, but retain a sense of local accountability and ownership at the same time."

KEY LEARNING POINTS

» Thinking globally and acting locally requires a regular exchange of ideas, experiences, and insights between central and local operations that is genuinely two-way.

» To acquire the skills, knowledge, and personal attributes to maintain this balance, staff will have to take part in a training program that is designed and run to international standards, and may entail them relocating either briefly or for longer periods of time.

» The seamlessness that this is designed to foster may be undermined by local social traditions, prevailing national management customs, ideological beliefs, or government policies that will have to be factored into the design of any training initiative and responded to.

FURTHER READING

Ulrich, D. & Stewart Black, J. (1999) "The new frontier of global HR," in P. Joynt & B. Morton (eds) *The Global HR Manager*. Institute of Personnel and Development, London.

Wetlaufer, S. (2000) "Common sense and conflict: an interview with Disney's Michael Eisner." *Harvard Business Review*, January – February.

Evolution: From Feudal Posts to Fast-track Projects

The term "global" to describe any aspect of management practice is little more than 15 years old. Prior to the 1990s, a form of "global training and development" did exist but it wasn't called that; instead, it was known by the name of "expatriate training." Moreover, it wasn't targeted at the whole workforce in an integrated, cross-functional organization; rather, it was confined to a small elite.

This chapter will trace how expatriate training developed in the decades immediately preceding the last 15 years, when global management concepts emerged. It will also show how, in the 1980s, a move away from old-style, long-term expatriate assignments to one-off projects and training that were linked to fast-track career schemes heralded the strategies used to support these concepts.

The next chapter ("Evolution: Towards a Global Learning Organization") will trace how a top-down transfer of TQM-inspired knowledge and technology was replaced over the initial period of global expansion by a two-way exchange of ideas and insights in the wake of "think global, act local" strategies.

The changeover period has been remarkably short. Nor are all these strategies mutually exclusive. Expatriate briefings, top-down technology transfer, and two-way exchanges of ideas and knowledge can, and do, simultaneously form part of a single organization's portfolio of training activities.

The evolution of global training and development from the twentieth century to the present day is represented as a timeline in the box below.

EVOLUTION OF GLOBAL TRAINING AND DEVELOPMENT OVER THE LAST 100 YEARS

» **Early twentieth century to 1970s:** Multinationals consist of loosely federated subsidiaries or local plants and representative offices. Responsibility highly devolved to local managers. Centrally supervised training confined to establishing pool of suitable expatriates. All other training undertaken locally.

» **1980s:** Corporate structure in state of flux. Long-term expatriates no longer appropriate or too costly. Short-term expatriates used for emergencies or special projects. Cross-cultural training replaces information briefings.

» **Early 1990s**: Rapid expansion into the emerging markets of Latin America, post-communist Central and Eastern Europe, and reformist Asia. Transfer of centrally developed knowledge, technology, and concepts a key competitive factor. All key local staff trained in new techniques, either locally or centrally. Managers and supervisors are the vanguard of new missions and business philosophies.

» **Late 1990s to early twenty-first century**: Top-down technology and knowledge transfer replaced by bottom-up exchange of ideas and experience, as the concept of thinking globally but acting locally takes hold. Intranet and peer-based learning support this process. International managers selected and trained to be experts in learning as much as in firm-specific technology or methodologies.

THE EXPATRIATE AS FEUDAL LORD

"People seem compelled to build walls, between themselves and others which, above all, slow things down," wrote Jack Welch in General Electric's 1994 annual report. But at the start of the twentieth century rather than at its conclusion, it wasn't people that built the walls but geography, technology, and tariff-based legislation.

The first multinationals were exclusively manufacturers. US foreign direct investment (FDI) statistics show that they first appeared in the world economy in the mid-nineteenth century and that businesses such as the sewing machine firm Singer and the electrical company Siemens were the pioneers.

By the time of World War I, multinational enterprise was a well-entrenched feature of the world economy. Manufacturers, most notably Ford, still dominated by the ranks of multinationals, were swelled by mining, exploration, and extraction companies like Royal Dutch Shell and De Beers.

International business activity grew vigorously in the 1920s, slowed down in the depressed and war-torn 1930s and 1940s, and then staged a heroic recovery in the 1950s, when it began a period of rapid growth which (albeit with fluctuations) has been sustained to the present day.

Little globally focused training took place during this period. Prior to 1945, FDI was undertaken exclusively from the developed world and was largely directed at the developing world, principally in the exploitation of primary products and services – gas and oil extraction, product export, local manufacturing, and so on.

English-speaking countries dominated. Britain was the world's largest investor, accounting for around 40 percent of the world's FDI in 1938, closely followed by the United States. The straightforward nature of the task of local managers – supervising the extraction of basic commodities or the manufacture of products for use at home or elsewhere in the world – required little conversational ability in another language and almost no cross-cultural skills in the sense that we know them today. All operations followed the "scientific" methods advocated by F.W. Taylor and Frank Gilbreth, in which work was broken down into tasks, and tasks into separate movements, so as to foster maximum efficiency.

A long way from Damascus (old Arab saying)

Local managers, anywhere in the world, ran the process rather than led the people. The growing need to establish or maintain representative corporate offices in newly independent countries, the sustained operations of the oil and gas exploration companies, and the explosion of infrastructure development in the Middle East and South Asia following the rise in oil prices in the 1970s required a cadre of expatriates who were both psychologically and professionally independent and self-sustaining.

These expats – field officers, engineers, construction workers, sales reps – operated semi-detached from the parent company. Aside from the most senior country executives, they were not drawn from the company's main management or professional workforce. When they moved post, they did so from one expatriate job to another. Their progress was not part of any integrated career management system. They worked, and lived, on rigs and construction sites and in field offices that were not part of the local social structure of the host country and had their own distinctive "frontier" culture. Interestingly, a very similar cadre of expatriate field officers, with the same semi-detached relation to their parent organization, run the local operations of non-government organizations such as Save the Children, Oxfam, Médecins sans Frontières, and the Red Cross today. (For further discussion of field officers, see Chapter 6.)

To the extent that there was any cross-cultural training at this point, it was how the individual (and his or her spouse and children if the job permitted the family to relocate) might manage the limited interaction they would have with local people without causing offense or misunderstanding. The emphasis of specialist agencies like the UK's Employment Conditions Abroad and the US Peace Corps was to provide *briefings* rather than training. These covered essential information on what schools or transport were available to foreigners, which local customs or religious beliefs were most likely to impact on their daily lives, and which climatic and health issues would need to be resolved. They did not cover the intricacies of running a cross-cultural project team or retaining and motivating local staff.

THE EXPATRIATE AS STOPGAP

By the mid-1980s, the expatriate population was beginning to change. The worldwide recession of 1981–2 resulted in widespread unemployment in host counties, leading to stiff local restrictions. The sheer costs of relocation for the parent company were making expatriates a corporate luxury. Educational standards in many developing countries had improved sufficiently to reduce the need for "imported technology." The recession had hit the construction industry particularly hard. Teams of workers were not being sent abroad in the numbers they were before.

During this intermediate stage of international employment, most expatriates were sent either on "first-aid missions" and short-term projects, or to fill very senior positions. The people who filled these posts were not the old-hand career expats of the previous decades, but inexperienced recruits from the in-house workforce.

As a result, selection methods for expats were increasingly integrated with systematic training designed to weed out those candidates who lacked the ability to cope with the stresses of an intense assignment, and provide likely recruits with a broader range of cultural skills than would ever have been provided to their predecessors.

Batting on the Bafa

Experiential learning made its first appearance. Bafa Bafa, the game in which participants role-play locals and expatriates in a variety of situations, is a good example. Originally developed for use with American air force personnel about to take up extended overseas postings, it was found to be equally effective for executives in the private sector. It gives those who have never worked with foreigners or been overseas a good taste of what personal and professional issues they may have to confront. For those with more international experience, it provides an opportunity to stop and analyze, and turn experience to better use.

More time was now spent preparing employees for the mental effects of leaving home and going abroad, rather than quickly forgotten facts about climate and politics. For the first time, training and selection were predicated on the results of psychological inventories. A pioneer in this field was the inventory developed specifically for expatriate selection and training by the US consulting firm Moran, Stahl & Boyer.

Initially undertaken on behalf of the Peace Corps, the overseas assignment inventory (OAI) allowed candidates to be measured against a selection of 17 "indicators of successful intercultural adjustment and performance," among others "a sense of humor," "attitudes towards drinking," and "attitudes towards drugs." Particularly valuable was the fact that the OAI didn't discriminate between men and women, and while developed for Anglo-Saxons was found to be equally effective for Hispanic and Oriental candidates.

Underskin diving

The need to collaborate with, rather than supervise, professionally educated local nationals meant that cross-cultural training also became a focus for expatriate training for the first time. Geert Hofstede, a former engineer, chief psychologist at IBM, and lecturer at INSEAD and IMD, co-founded the Institute for Research on Intercultural Cooperation in 1980 at Tilburg University, Holland. In 1985, he became professor of anthropology and international management at Maastrict University, also in Holland, teaching there until 1993.

Building on his close links with IBM, Hofstede surveyed 100,000 of the corporation's staff in 72 countries, looking at the differences caused by macro-cultures that impacted on IBM's already strong corporate culture. From this, Hofstede identified four dimensions governing national cultural diversity: uncertainty avoidance, power distance, masculinity–femininity, and individualism–collectivism. (For a more detailed analysis of the four dimensions, see Chapter 8.)

Individualism–collectivism, for example, is the extent to which a society favors individual over collective action and effort. The more affluent a country becomes, he finds, the more it moves towards individualism. There is also a tendency for Protestant Christian societies to be individualist and Catholic ones to be more group-oriented. Building on this spiritual underpinning, Hofstede identified a fifth dimension, Confucian dynamism, to explain the rapid development of many Asian "tiger" economies, looking at the effects of Confucian teachings and ethics on thrift, perseverance, a sense of shame, and a belief in hierarchy.

THE EXPATRIATE AS HIGH-FLYER

Parallel with the move towards shorter expatriate assignments, the fast-track schemes that had been the cornerstone of large corporations' succession planning for several decades began to take on a more international flavor.

An essential feature of fast-track schemes is that the career progression of young management talent is structured around a series of cross-functional projects or assignments. These projects are supposed to allow the individual to build up an overview of the business and develop a network of relationships that will underpin his or her authority as a senior manager. (For a fuller discussion of this topic, see the ExpressExec guide *Management Development*.)

Icarus ascending

Yet – perhaps reflecting how late large corporations were to take internationalism seriously – the nature of these projects was still surprisingly parochial in the mid-1980s. At IBM, where Geert Hofstede conducted his research, the seven specific characteristics used to identify candidates for fast-track development included being "credible at all levels" and "cross-functionally aware" but not "credible in all *countries*" or "cross- *culturally* aware".

Only 25 percent of IBM's UK expatriates in 1987 were in overseas assignments specifically to develop their potential as senior managers. This reflected the findings of a study by Italy's Ambrosetti Consulting Group in the same year, which found that 80 percent of the UK directors surveyed did not speak a second language and that 40 percent had no international experience at all.

By the end of the decade, this level of neglect was becoming difficult to sustain. European Union statistics show that the number of inter-country mergers and acquisitions involving EU-based companies tripled between 1983 and 1987, and quadrupled in the following five years.

The immediate effect was the internationalization of existing boards. In the summer of 1988, for example, the top retailer Storehouse had just appointed a Frenchman, Michel Julien, as its chief executive. Schoichi Saba, Toshiba's chief executive, was sitting on the board of UK chemical giant ICI in company with an American and a West German. Nestlé had just appointed an American to its board of 15 directors, joining two Frenchmen, a German, and a Spaniard. Forbo, a Swiss firm, was pioneering the concept of a "truly" global board. It was composed of directors from all the 10 countries where it had factories. Meetings were conducted in English, French, or German.

Boundary bouncing

However, it was also becoming clear that – as partners, competitors, customers, and suppliers were all crossing geographical boundaries – both up-and-coming senior executives and technical front-line managers would need internationalizing too. As a consequence, both existing and new fast-track schemes were upgraded to encompass selection from the broader pool of international candidates that were now becoming available. These were supported by general management development initiatives that provided international experience, team-building exercises that extended beyond national boundaries, and better use of employee communications and events that fostered a truly international corporate culture.

A good example was Olivetti's "No Frontiers" program, which targeted systems support managers. The program was launched in

1986, specifically in response to the increasingly international business of the company's clients. The third intake, in 1989, included 13 different nationalities in a group of 58. A careful assessment was made of global needs. A worldwide campaign was run entirely in English. Recruiters in the individual subsidiaries were all carefully trained by headquarters instructors to look for the same qualities, and to give them the same emphasis.

All successful candidates were then flown in to undergo the "No Frontiers" training program at the company's headquarters in Ivrea, Italy. The program was designed to foster close personal networks as well as providing essential technical expertise. "Candidates form strong bonds while studying together," said Tirad Sorooshian, a projects training manager on the program. "Back at their jobs, they phone each other to talk over problems and help each other."

CONCLUSION: EMPLOYERS AT THE GLOBAL BRINK

The techniques on initiatives like the "No Frontiers" program were cutting-edge but the rationale was little different from the old-style expatriate briefings of the 1960s and 1970s. "Going global" was a matter of strategic intent requiring an international perspective among the board, the senior management team, and key professional workers. When companies were catapulted into the real complexities of acquiring or collaborating with partners in developing countries, they found that the necessary change in perspective was organization-wide. The global company had arrived and, as the next chapter will show, the training challenge was awesome.

KEY LEARNING POINTS

» The management of early expatriates was a matter of selection rather than training. Get the recruitment right and all you needed to provide in the way of training was briefings about local customs, conditions, and facilities.

» This changed as long-term expatriate posts became too expensive to maintain and were rendered redundant by the emergence of a better-trained, qualified workforce. Executives sent from the parent company had to work with these new workers rather than over them, and this required (for the first time) an accurate understanding of cross-cultural forces that might lead to tensions or misunderstandings.

» The need for senior executives and key professional workers to acquire an international perspective of business led to short-term expatriate assignments or overseas projects being linked to fast-track development schemes. Gradually this "exposure" to international environments was percolated downwards to training schemes aimed at front-line consultants and technicians.

» Until the early 1990s, however, global training and development schemes were not deemed to encompass the whole workforce.

FURTHER READING

Hofstede, G. (2001) *Culture's Consequences: Comparing values, behaviors, institutions, and organizations across nations*, 2nd edn. Sage Publications, London and Thousand Oaks, California.

Iles, F. (1994) *Moving Asian Managers in Asia-Pacific: Structuring an appropriate expatriate package*. Economist Intelligence Unit/Wyatt Company, Hong Kong.

Hofstede, G. (1988) "Confucius and economic growth: new trends in culture's consequences." *Organisational Dynamics*, **16**:4.

Hogg, C. (1991) "World role for business players." *The Times*, April 11.

Hogg, C. & Syrett, M. (1989) "Getting the right management for 1992." *Director*, March.

Evolution: Towards a Global Learning Organization

- » The emergence of the regional expatriate
- » The international manager as champion of quality
- » The international manager as resource gatherer
- » Key learning points
- » Further reading

Globalism proper hit the business world in the early 1990s, as the twin events of communism's collapse in Central and Eastern Europe and its reform in China and Vietnam opened up a third of the world's untapped economies to free-market capitalism.

The tentative reforms made to parochial management development initiatives the previous decade were now transformed and expanded as a result of three by-products of the very rapid expansion into unexplored commercial territories in countries like Hungary, Poland, Russia, China, and India.

THE EMERGENCE OF THE REGIONAL EXPATRIATE

The first by-product was a vastly more complex cultural infrastructure. Building on the work of Holland's Geert Hofstede, Asia's leading expert on Chinese business culture Gordon Redding, then director of the business school at the University of Hong Kong, identified three very different social dynamics in Asia-Pacific that directly influenced the relationship international corporations had with locally recruited managers.

» *Post-Confucian*: These societies inherited a long tradition of highly refined and systematized stratification and then disowned it before replacing it with a system based on personal achievement through education and career success. Japan, South Korea, Singapore, Taiwan, and Hong Kong fall into this category.
» *Post-communist*: These societies acted with aggressive and destructive egalitarian zeal to level all social classes to the same point. But by failing to erect alternative systems to define and determine status, they leave people to claim influence through political position. China and Vietnam can be classified as such.
» *Post-colonial*: Although previously colonized, these communities have retained their older social orders. Much of this is invisible to the outsider and rests on criteria such as family history, landholding, education, and connections. Indonesia, Malaysia, and the Philippines are in this grouping.

Thai people, for example, place the family first, school mates second, and employers a poor third. It is something that puts Thai managers in a difficult position if pressure from relatives and friends conflicts with their employers' commercial interests. Equally, North American or European notions of empowerment may clash with Indonesian values of harmony and loyalty, which say that upsetting the whole for the sake of the individual is counterproductive.

When in Rome...

The second by-product was a dramatically increased need for regional expatriates. Companies found very quickly that targeting and understanding the needs of an increasingly affluent mass market was better undertaken by managers recruited and developed locally and then circulated around the region than by outsiders, however authentic their lingual skills and regional or local knowledge.

What this means in practice was spelt out in a survey of 100 multinationals based in Asia by the Economist Intelligence Unit in conjunction with the Wyatt Company in 1994. The report confirmed the rising presence of locally recruited expatriates. In the previous five years, locally recruited expatriates were forecast to increase by more than 65 percent while overseas postings filled by North Americans or Europeans had dropped by 20 percent.

However the survey also vividly portrayed the scale of the training, and the career management challenge this presented. Seventy-five percent of the expatriates employed by the sample were on their first assignment, and the speed and scale with which locally recruited expatriates were being assigned was bankrupting the resources and expertise of regional and local HR to provide them with effective induction or preparation – a failing exacerbated by the fact that until then many companies, Western and Asian alike, saw locally recruited expatriates as an attraction because they were cheaper to employ.

THE INTERNATIONAL MANAGER AS CHAMPION OF QUALITY

The third by-product of the economic revolution in the post-communist world was a mismatch between the business concepts that had been built up by multinationals in North America and Europe in the 1980s and the more traditional management practices that were still in place in developing countries, which were more redolent of Western business culture in the 1950s.

Eastern philosophy, Western orthodoxy

The West, ironically in deference to post-war Japanese manufacturing methods, had undergone a revolution in the decade before communism collapsed. The total quality philosophy of W. Edwards Deming and Joseph Juran had been universally subscribed to, and adapted (albeit disjointedly) to service as well as manufacturing operations. Toyota's concept of lean manufacturing, coupled with delayering in an attempt to cut costs, had resulted in slimmer management structures where fast promotion was based on a proven ability to meet very tight performance targets rather than status or long service.

Western companies now attempted to impose these reforms on post-communist and post-colonial societies that were not ready for it. Much of the mass management development activity that took place during this period was designed to grapple with the cultural disconnections that occurred.

For example, the induction and preparation required by locally recruited expatriates was significantly higher than that conventionally provided to their North American and European counterparts. Contrary to the rather naïve assumptions made by Western executives, expatriates from one part of the region were more likely to encounter racism and hostility from local staff in another than if they were "white."

Early expectations that new mainland Chinese operations could be resourced by Hong Kong nationals, for example, were dashed when it became clear that discrimination against Cantonese-speaking southerners everywhere other than their homelands was intense – and that the hostility was enthusiastically reciprocated. The same applied to Malaysian and Singaporean recruits, even if they were recruited from long-standing Chinese diaspora communities.

In addition, Asian managers generally were more reluctant to take up expatriate postings for a whole host of reasons that included a lack of appropriate schooling and cultural facilities, more extensive extended family responsibilities, and a widely held perception (reinforced by experience) that expatriate postings in Asia were "assignments to oblivion."

The experiences of one highly qualified Indonesian manager, interviewed in the Economist Intelligence Unit report, illustrates what happened when he was transferred to Hong Kong:

> "I was looking for proper logistics and support when I arrived. I was expecting someone would be delegated to look after me and would be specifically trained to handle the difficult problems I would encounter. In fact, the manager assigned to look after my interests was not trained to look after the needs of third country nationals. He gave me the sense that he was feeling 'You are Indonesian. You shouldn't be here, but since you are I suppose I better give you some help.' There was no dedicated human resource professional to support him and no company guidelines for him to fall back on."

Similarly, the concept that managers in a quality-based corporation should be able to work across geographical boundaries and functional divides, and be promoted solely on ability, did not sit well in post-Confucian and post-colonial societies where status based on age and background lurked beneath the surface. A study of 60 multinationals by the Poon Kam Kai Institute of Management in Hong Kong in 1995 found that total quality management (TQM) was being undermined by the dislike and unwillingness of local Chinese managers to work on an equal basis with counterparts who were either from different functions or junior to them.

As Derek Welch, general manager of business development for Courtaulds in the early 1990s, comments: "Western management practice demands that companies have delayered structures in which managers and professionals are promoted on the basis of their measured performance. This did not fit in well in Asian countries where managers have traditionally achieved status on the basis of their family or schooling; or others where seniority is linked to your standing in government or the local community."

One slogan is as good as another

Nor was this cultural mismatch confined to Asia. The experiences of General Electric (GE) when it acquired the Hungarian light bulb manufacturer Tungsram following the collapse of the Comecon economy is fairly typical of what occurred in a post-communist society. Under the supervision of production director Don McKenna, time between order and delivery at Tungsram plants was slashed – from 90 days in 1990 to 32 days in 1994. Breakages on the production line were cut over the same period from a staggering one in two in pre-GE days to near world standards.

The acid test of the reforms, however, lay in GE's ability to promote teamwork and Western-style project management in a culture previously reliant on rigid demarcation. "Our world totally changed," says project manager Tibor Fricsan, who saw Tungsram's layers of management cut from 11 to 3 in less than two years. Tamas Palopia, senior leadership technology director, agrees: "People who were used to a hierarchical structure where the boss gave the orders had to adjust in a very short period of time to the idea that decisions are taken by teams and not individuals."

Much of this could have been said by any line manager in North America and Europe during the TQM revolution in the West a few years earlier. However, the fact that Hungary and other Central European countries had only just emerged from 40 years of a command economy added a new twist to the adjustment. Under the socialists, exhortations to greater productivity were seen as political slogans to be ignored or bypassed. The result was that, while GE executives regarded phrases such as "empowerment" and "a culture of winning" as articles of faith, to supervisors and workers on the shop floor they bore a confusing similarity to the slogans of the old order.

"Providing junior managers and supervisors with the necessary team-building and project leadership skills was the easy part," says Bob Lubecky, who joined Tungsram in 1992 as director of technology from GE's halogen engineering business in the US. "It was getting over the message that the need to work across boundaries and break down internal barriers were not words you put on a banner or a factory poster and forgot, but things you put into practice in your day to day work, that was the real challenge."

THE INTERNATIONAL MANAGER AS RESOURCE GATHERER

Much of the knowledge and skills transfer in the first wave of globalism was one-way. Locally recruited managers such as Tibor Fricsan and Tamas Palopia at Tungsram were acting as brokers, gatekeepers, and pulse-takers for products, services, and ways of working that had been developed by their employers in another world. The training they received, in common with all other employees, was to conduct business the company way.

However, the mid-1990s philosophy of "think global, act local" and the accompanying emphasis on innovation as a strategic competitive capability have reversed the knowledge flow. Now, effective management development is as much about capturing and tapping the hidden insights of local front-line managers as imposing centrally devised values and ways of working.

Dave Ulrich of the University of Michigan's Business School, the latest "globalism guru," defines the balance in this way:

» being able to determine core activities from non-core activities;
» achieving consistency while allowing flexibility;
» building global brand equity while honoring local customs;
» obtaining leverage (bigger is better) while achieving focus (smaller is better);
» sharing learning and creating new knowledge; and
» engendering global perspective while ensuring local accountability.

Ulrich cites the dilemma facing Disney in applying its core principle that the company's theme parks should be a "clean, safe and enjoyable experience for families." Working on the basis that alcohol was not compatible with a safe, fun experience for families, Disney banned alcohol in all its parks. But visitors to its park in Paris complained, so the top team had to decide whether its assumptions were applicable in Europe.

"To an extent, this was about being able to distinguish ends from means," Ulrich explains. "For Disney, the end was a clean, safe, fun experience for families. An alcohol ban was a means to this end. But it had been a means for so long that it had become an end in itself. Success on this issue came only when executives recognized that regional differences required adaptation to reach the desired global ends. Consequently, beer and wine are now served at Disneyland, Paris."

Ulrich also makes the point that while adherence to the company's core principles can be achieved by focused recruitment, thus achieving the first aim of thinking globally, sharing and creating new knowledge, the gateway to being able to act locally, can only be achieved through management development. This has become truer in recent years with the emergence of strategic alliances, where knowledge and technology transfer is a key benefit.

Examples of globally applied programs that aim to exchange and capture new knowledge are included in Chapters 5 and 7. They include Standard Chartered Bank, which found that internal benchmarking between its European and Asian operations threw up more transferable good practice on customer service than studying the techniques of its competitors; Lufthansa, whose management development expertise acted as the lynchpin in its alliance with United Airlines, Air Canada, Varig (of Brazil), Scandinavian Airlines (SAS), and Thai Airlines among others; and BMW, where management development initiatives underpin cross-national senior executive succession planning.

All of these initiatives are designed from the principle that local operations and global headquarters have something to teach and something to learn from each other. The creative tension governing the exchange is delicate and – a point stressed by Dave Ulrich – needs expert HR input both in judging which capabilities are required to achieve globalization and localization and how these can be developed.

"If globalization meant integration and worldwide standardization, or if it meant separation and adaptation, people wouldn't be confused," he says. "We know how to standardize. We know how to adapt. What we find difficult is doing both at the same time."

KEY LEARNING POINTS

» Global management strategies have moved, very fast, from being an ancillary to the recruitment and transfer of expatriates to the principal means of achieving commonly held standards and values that are seamless and easily transferable across geographical boundaries.

» In the early years of globalism, when establishing common quality standards was a priority, the process was a top-down affair, established through "cascading" workshops and seminars that established a consensus in one layer of management before moving onto the next (lower) one.

» Now, the dynamic is becoming more bottom-up and sideways. The diverse views held by a global workforce, made up of people with different or locally informed perspectives of both the business and its markets, are being tapped through seminars that act as think tanks and brainstorms. Learning through social serendipity rather than codified rules is the main goal.

FURTHER READING

Redding, G. and Armitage, C. (1993) *Management Development in Asia-Pacific: Moulding managers for success*. Economist Intelligence Unit, Hong Kong.

Syrett, M. (1994) "Global firms act and think local in hiring Asian staff." *South China Morning Post*, February 9.

Syrett, M. & Kingston, K. (1995) "GE's Hungarian light switch." *Management Today*, April.

Ulrich, D. & Stewart Black, J. (1999) "The new frontier of global HR," in P. Joynt & B. Morton (eds) *The Global HR Manager*. Institute of Personnel and Development, London.

The E-Dimension

"The on-line self is supported by neither time, space nor body, and yet it is unmistakably present," quoted an early Website designed by Mintel. The nature and presence of the online self is an abiding obsession for all training in the Internet age, but no more so than in the global arena where the Internet's capacity to cut across all boundaries has transformed what is and is not possible.

The technology used as recently as the 1980s for what were then termed distance-learning programs would now be seen as at best intermediate and at worst downright primitive. Individuals used a combination of a text (to provide the basic principles of the concepts being learned) with videos (to provide visual case studies) and audio tapes (to provide input by lecturers and experts). The text was termed "interactive" but this meant that it was integrated with other components of the package rather than with concepts picked up through human interaction.

SUMMERTIME BLUES

To provide a necessary element of human interaction, individuals were encouraged, or required, to attend summer schools or local learning centers, where they could meet tutors and other students on the program. They also needed access to a well-resourced library to undertake self-managed desk research. This was fine if the necessary infrastructure was in place but broke down very quickly if the distances between resource centers were too great.

It does not take too much imagination to grasp the implications of this if companies or business schools attempted to apply these methods to a cadre of students who lived in territories with radically contrasting levels of educational resources. The UK's Open University, one of the pioneers of distance learning, had accepted by the end of the 1980s that the ability of their students to successfully complete their studies was significantly greater, or shorter, in countries like Belgium and the Netherlands, where urban living was high and access to libraries and study centers was easy, than it was in rural regions where the distances between facilities were much greater.

Even in relatively sophisticated worldwide centers, the ability of either companies or schools to maintain the necessarily high standards of support required by distance learning students was very patchy. A survey of 24 institutions offering distance learning in Hong Kong by the Territory's Open Learning Institute and the Australian Education Centre in 1994, for example, found that 33 percent failed to offer students regular study sessions, 33 percent of those that offered study sessions failed to offer academic feedback outside tutorials, 25 percent that did offer this kind of feedback took over a month to respond to students, and 50 percent of them all provided no library facilities for necessary desk research.

DISTANT HORIZONS TO VIRTUAL RELATIONSHIPS

Once the Cold War barriers were down and commercial expansion to previously untouched and largely rural regions like Russia, China, and Vietnam were on the cards, the ability of old-style distance learning broke down completely. Without the human interaction brought about by regular attendance at study centers, the programs were little more than sophisticated correspondence courses.

Traditional providers went to great lengths to bridge the gap. By 1995, the Open University Business School (OUBS) had set up 90 study centers in Russia supported by more than 100 tutors. The local tutors recruited for the task attended intensive residential schools in Russia and the UK to enable them to understand and apply new management theory to the Russian managerial model. But even in this case, the OUBS centers were largely confined to urban areas and were mostly based in Western cities that could offer the physical and human resources needed to set up an effective distance-learning infrastructure.

The availability of inexpensive Internet technology changed all this. Overnight the constraints that had hampered the expansion of distance learning to developing economies were removed – provided the student could gain regular access to a terminal. The development of company-based intranets also meant that large corporations with the right internal HR expertise could launch their own worldwide training initiatives in a way that simply would not have been possible a decade before.

An early pioneer was Standard Chartered Bank. In the early 1990s, Standard Chartered launched a series of management education initiatives aimed at transforming the bank from one run predominately by expatriates to one managed by a truly international team.

Although British-owned, the bank's main presence is in Africa and Asia. Standard Chartered operates as a high-street bank in many of these regions – prior to the transfer of sovereignty of Hong Kong to China in 1997, it was one of the issuers of the local currency – but it sees its main growth in the future in providing top-grade financial services to international corporations, something that requires highly educated professional teams operating to consistent international standards.

Accordingly, it designed its own Master of Business Administration (MBA) program in such a way that it could be delivered to, and studied by, managers from a wide variety of functions in countries around the world. In the first intake, in 1991, 18 managers from 12 countries took part, ranging from the chief financial officer in Tokyo and the senior strategic officer in Hong Kong to branch managers in Sidcup in the UK and Kuala Lumpur in Malaysia.

The program was designed and delivered by the UK's Henley Management College. Participants were provided with a portable personal computer to help them communicate with each other, their tutors, and in-company trainers through Henley's global conferencing system.

THE HOLY GRAIL OF INTERACTION

The availability of Henley's global conferencing software made it possible for the first time for groups of students in different locations to undertake at a distance the kind of sophisticated group work that previously would only have been practical during a residential summer school or in an in-company training center.

A study group in Asia, for instance, might be set the task of looking at the potential market for sophisticated financial services in central China. The group would then liaise with each other by computer, reach their conclusions, and report back their findings to all other participants. Potentially, the whole transaction could be virtual.

"The holy grail for us is to bring about an imaginative interaction between participants which leads to effective problem solving, decision making and the development of new ideas," says Dominic Swords, director of corporate qualification programs at Henley Management College. "New technologies such as groupware, discussion databases and the Internet increase the sense of intimacy between ourselves and the participants. They have replaced more bureaucratic forms of communication which made it hard to maintain the sharing process when participants had dispersed to different parts of the world."

Yet at the time of the first intake, there were still felt to be limitations on how much of the total program could be conducted virtually. Each intake on the Standard Chartered program continued to meet three times a year in the UK, Malaysia, and Hong Kong, and each study group met at least once a quarter. Dominic Swords stresses that the degree of intimacy participants maintain over the Internet was only possible because of the bonding that takes place during the residential courses. "We use these courses to undertake teambuilding and cross-cultural work, including outdoor training," he says. "The lesson we are learning again and again is that sophisticated learning over the Web can only be fostered through a face to face encounter."

Michael Earl, professor of information management at London Business School agrees: "The one thing technology has yet to reproduce is the tacit language brought about by close human contact." For this reason, Earl argues that technology has yet to replace the role played by the guru or "inspired teacher" as he puts it. "Technology can substitute the dissemination of expert knowledge, but it cannot reproduce the evangelical process of a creative individual who paints a picture of a promised land and charts a road that helps managers reach it."

He might have done well to insert the little word "yet" at the end of the last sentence. The issue of whether people can develop the kind of intimacy over the Net that experts like Dominic Swords and Michael Earl feel is necessary for close group work and for inspired teachers to go on inspiring is no longer a matter of technological capability. The technology, as we have seen, already exists. It is a matter of an individual's comfort with the medium and, as a new generation of workers brought up on computer (and mobile phone text) interactions enters the global labor force, this cultural assimilation is likely to increase.

NEW BOUNDARIES, NEW BORDERLINES

Earl and Swords' schools have already been pushing out the boundaries. London Business School's semi-detached relationship with one of its top academic stars, Gary Hamel, has been fostered by Hamel's contribution to seminars, MBA class discussions, and executive courses via videoconferencing software. This medium enables him to make the kind of real-time observations and (to use Earl's terminology) "charting to a promised land" that a evangelical guru would normally make face to face.

Henley's experiments with videoconferencing have also been geared up by a distance-learning MBA program it launched with Cable & Wireless in the late 1990s. The only distance-learning MBA focusing specifically on the communications industry, it is designed to provide participants with the opportunity to study for an MBA without a career break. Some 85 managers from 20 countries, and of 18 nationalities, are currently studying for the qualification, supported by Lotus Notes software giving them access to the faculty and the opportunity to network with each other. Networking at a distance is reinforced by residential study sessions allowing students to meet with colleagues and peers around the world from a variety of organizations and functional backgrounds.

Under the curriculum, the foundation assignment examining the basics of strategy is followed by a module on managing people and two week-long residential sessions on managing telecommunications, covering issues like the global telecommunications environment, working in an internationally networked environment, and new business development in the telecommunications industry. This, together with a series of modules on managing marketing, performance, and financial resources, leads to the student being granted a diploma in management.

In the final part of the program, which leads to an MBA, participants use the knowledge provided by two further modules covering strategic direction and business transformation (the second studied outside the UK) to undertake a project focusing on how to manage telecommunications strategically, tackling issues such as the impact of regulatory changes, the effects of globalization and technology in strategic planning, and how to implement strategy in a telecommunications organization.

The whole program is designed to take 2.5 years to complete, involving 1200 hours of study and 5 weeks of residential study. Managers from a wide range of functions have been drawn together.

Current students include a support engineer from Hong Kong, a business development manager from the Maldives, a finance account manager from France, an HR manager from the UK, and a project manager from Russia.

The sheer scope of the project has limited the number of times that students can meet and obliged Henley's distance-learning experts to use videoconferencing against their better instincts, with results that astonished them. "In our development of distance learning, we are always driven by the standards of the company," said program director Colin Carnell a year into the project.

"Cable & Wireless use videoconferencing on a global basis and it was a requirement of the contract that we incorporate this technology into our learning design. Our knowledge and understanding of how videoconferencing can be used to conduct 'live teaching' has been given a huge boost. If you had showed me at the beginning of last year how far we would have reached by this time as a result, I would have found it hard to believe."

Why was videoconferencing so successful on the program? Because, as Carnell subsequently acknowledged, its widespread use at Cable & Wireless as a routine communications medium in a company where telecommunications itself was second nature meant that the discomfort normally exhibited by managers of the same age in other companies simply did not exist.

BEST PRACTICE: SHELL INTERNATIONAL EXPLORATION AND PRODUCTION (SIEP)

The full potential of Web technology, as a conduit of essential knowledge for all staff and not just managers, is illustrated by the global knowledge communities set up by SIEP following a seminal report, *New Ways of Working*, in 1998.

There are currently 11 of them and between them they cover all of the company's core businesses, plus support functions such as HR, IT, finance, and procurement. The founder of the initiative, Arjan van Unnik, wanted to find a way in which an individual in one part of Shell's global operations, say in Nigeria, could tap into potential solutions to a problem that might be held in another part, say the North Sea, without time-consuming paperwork and bureaucracy.

Prior to 1998, SIEP had used a telephone-style directory of experts, but the information listed tended to be general, whereas problems that need solving are usually very specific. It was impossible for any expert to anticipate all the problems he or she might be able to solve in a directory-style entry. The answer, hit upon by van Unnik, was to find a way for people to broadcast their problems to the right community.

Hitting on a dedicated intranet as the most efficient medium was the easy part. Defining what constituted the "right" community was the key to the success of the project. Too large, and the problem would get lost. Too small, and people would have to belong to and tap into several groups to reach the person with the expertise they needed.

From little acorns

After experimenting with a number of options, van Unnik settled on the current balance of size, expertise, and accessibility. Each community begins with a seed group – about 25 people who are enthusiastic and have ideas to exchange. This group generates the initial traffic. From responses to this traffic, they then invite the next layer of people to join in – and so on. The cascade dynamic is predicated on the principal that it is always existing users that bring in more users and that members are not determined by diktat. An important corollary is that, from the seed group upward, the community is global.

The optimum size of group is also not predetermined. SIEP's core business groups have 3000 to 4000 members each, while support functions like the HR community set up in 2001 have only 500–1000. This does not just reflect the relative size of the functions but the nature of the information and the people who are sharing it. The engineers who work in the core business come from a culture where sharing information is second nature. It's also hard factual stuff. As van Unnik comments, "You extract oil or you don't."

Each community has a moderator, or coordinator, who is responsible for controlling content and traffic flow. Coordinators encourage people to contribute and ensure questions are posed, and answers proffered, quickly and in an accessible manner. In the operating companies there are also individuals called hub coordinators, responsible for building up each community at a local level.

The initiative has more than paid for itself in money-saving solutions. When Shell Brazil needed help retrieving broken tools from a borehole, engineers turned to the global knowledge community for help and within 24 hours, with its help, were able to identify a strategy to save the well and with it a US$7mn investment. A manager in Shell Malaysia was able to shut down a gas turbine cheaply and effectively using methods pioneered by teams in Australia and the US that, but for the global knowledge network, would not have been captured and codified. Altogether, van Unnik estimates that Shell has saved US$200mn through knowledge sharing of this kind.

Sitting over the virtual shoulder

But it isn't just financial savings that have emerged from the initiative. Almost from the start, it became clear that these global networks are excellent personal development tools – a source of peer-based learning that, van Unnik argues, beats courses and books.

As the larger, more developed communities have gathered more traffic, they have amassed a huge body of material. This archive remains at the fingertips of every single community member. As a result, people have started using the networks as libraries. Search tools mean they can find out if anyone had a similar problem, look at what's been suggested and, if they still don't get a precise answer, put together a list of people whom they can contact directly.

The global knowledge network is closely integrated with another Web-based personal development initiative, the Shell Open University. This now has 11,000 registered users and offers 600 courses, some delivered online, some classroom-based, some delivered solely by Shell and some by external tutors who have a close relationship with the corporation.

In a classic example of how the feedback from internally generated database discussions, if properly captured, can be transformed into firm-specific concepts, the archive of practical experiences amassed by the SIEP global networks is providing Shell Open University courses with its own regularly updated learning materials. "We have had no need to write or update made for purpose case studies or scenarios," concludes van Unnik. "The material is there for the taking. The intervention made by professional trainers is minimal."

KEY LEARNING POINTS

» Internet-based learning has made group work and team assignments between course participants in different locations as potentially effective as if they were conducting them face to face.

» Individuals' comfort with the technology is the key. Most trainers use "blended" learning that combines face-to-face work (to establish an initial bond) with Internet exchanges (to sustain it). However, the composition of this blend will change with the recruitment of a new generation of workers, who have established and sustained relationships using advanced technology since they were children.

» Knowledge exchange and the creation of new ideas and concepts, so central to transnational business, is exceptionally effective using Internet technology. If combined with formal training, as in the case of the Shell Open University, it can provide a rich archive of firm-specific solutions and learning materials that can be regularly sourced, adapted, and updated.

FURTHER READING

Syrett, M. & Lammiman, J. (1999) *Management Development: Making the investment count*. Economist Books, London.

Carrington, L. (2002) "Oiling the wheels." *People Management*, June 27.

Syrett, M. (1997) "Changing the face of learning." *Director*, April.

Vicere, A.A. (2000) "Ten observations on e-learning." *Human Resource Planning*, November.

The State of the Art

» The multinational model: Devolution to managers in the field
» The global corporate model: Company-wide technology transfer
» The transnational company model: Knowledge exchange and bottom-up innovation
» Conclusion: Stripping away the emperor's clothes
» Key learning points
» Further reading

A good starting point for looking at the essential tasks of global training and development is the research of professors Sumantra Ghoshal of INSEAD and London Business School and Christopher Bartlett of Harvard Business School (see also Chapter 8).

Ghoshal and Bartlett identified four stages of globalism, each with its own organizational culture, command, and control dynamic.

1 *Multinationals*: These are essentially federations of multiple national companies loosely connected across borders and largely managed by expatriates sent from the center. In these companies, management authority is highly devolved with key decisions made by field or regional executives able to work across different cultures and trained to be self-sufficient.

2 *Global corporations*: These are similar to multinationals but have a less feudal structure. Subsidiaries or divisions are managed more closely from the center in a way that enables the corporation as a whole to benefit from economies of scale in manufacturing and distribution. In these companies, global postings and participation on senior executive courses run by prestigious international business schools are grafted onto existing high-flyer schemes (see Chapter 3). This ensures that senior executives who will shape the future strategy of the organization have a global perspective of its front-line operations.

3 *International companies*: These resemble multinationals but increasingly transfer their centrally produced technology and marketing expertise to their local businesses rather than vesting them in a central elite. These companies place locally recruited staff on centrally designed, and often centrally delivered, training programs to ensure that operations throughout the world offer services or products to a consistently high standard.

4 *Transnational companies:* The ideal end point according to Ghoshal and Bartlett, transnational companies take as their main goal the imperative identified by Percy Barnevik of Asea Brown Boveri that organizations need to "think global, act local." These firms combine local knowledge with a quick global market response. Knowledge transfer is more sophisticated, manufacturing and R&D are located in the most cost-efficient places and there is serious training and knowledge transfer to exploit unfamiliar markets.

As this chapter will show, training and development initiatives are usually a central mechanism to help companies move from one stage to another.

THE MULTINATIONAL MODEL: DEVOLUTION TO MANAGERS IN THE FIELD

In the modern world of globally integrated operations, the concept of career expatriates sent by the center to run local operations seems medieval. Yet there are still organizations who operate successfully in this framework.

Hong Kong-based trading companies, for example, have supported the growth of Asia's tiger economies for decades. Because they have often played an across-the-board role in developing regions with poor base infrastructures – most recently in post-Deng China – they encompass industries that would seem unrelated and totally lacking in synergy in the sophisticated economies of North America and Europe.

Closely following the multinational template identified by Ghoshal and Bartlett, management responsibility is highly devolved. Local executives in the field are given a great deal of operational discretion. Accountability from the center is largely confined to board-level financial reporting.

Jardines, previously Jardine Matheson, is typical. It operates in a patchwork of industries, including aviation and shipping, information technology, retailing, financial and property services, the restaurant business, security and environmental services, and engineering and construction.

Because the level of responsibility ceded to local managers is almost feudal, and therefore critical to fulfilling the strategy of company as a whole, Jardines has a strong commitment to training and development from the moment junior managers are recruited. Their progress is tracked and appraised regularly by a centralized "People Management" department. All managers follow a formal development program – which encompasses an induction and training program – within a month of their arrival, and a more comprehensive executive development program within three months of their arrival. These are followed by a series of courses covering more specialist topics at regular intervals during the next few years.

But in contrast to the past, when talented individuals were circulated around all the key industries in the early stages of their careers, trainees are now expected to build their careers within one industry sector. As Eleanor Ling, a director of Jardine Pacific, commented in the mid-1990s: "Getting to know the business you start in is a priority, and this may involve tasks in the first few months as basic as shifting stock in a supermarket or cleaning cars in a garage. But the focus on industry specialization also means that management trainees who make the grade win significant responsibility very fast. It is not uncommon for Jardines' managers to find themselves in charge of a unit or a business by their mid-twenties."

To ensure that their most promising managers are not poorly networked as a result, Jardines has created a number of forums that cut across the entire organization. An example is the Jardines Ambassadors' Program, formed in 1982 as part of the company's 150th anniversary celebrations. The purpose of the program is to reinforce Jardines' role in the community through a series of projects and fundraising events. Although the focus of the projects is charitable, the make-up of the people seconded to take part in them is designed to bring managers from different parts of the organization together, and to allow young professionals the opportunity to bring themselves to the notice of senior managers in an unpressured way.

THE GLOBAL CORPORATE MODEL: COMPANY-WIDE TECHNOLOGY TRANSFER

The contrast between the business culture of well-established economies in North America and the European Union, and those of emerging or rapidly developing ones in Eastern Europe, Asia, and Latin America, is not as deep-rooted as MBA-educated idealists would have us believe.

Western corporations were every bit as hierarchical, paternalist, prejudiced, and top-heavy as their counterparts in less developed parts of the world in the 1970s. What made the global expansion in the early 1990s so energetic (and often controversial) was that these corporations had just undergone a decade of internal revolution at home, based on concepts of total quality management and lean production imported (ironically) from Japan. And, like all new converts, they were evangelical in their enthusiasm to export it, in its Western form, to their newly acquired subsidiaries or joint-venture partners.

The result was, and still is, that global training and development strategies are partially founded on the need to transfer new production technology, sector-based knowledge, and management practices consistently throughout the company's worldwide network. This has been further encouraged by the establishment of international quality standards, which have to be acquired by local suppliers and distributors if they want to win work from newly established global corporations.

Empowerment China-style

Global corporations have generally undertaken the task in one of two ways. The first is on a local level. A good example was the cultural overhaul undertaken by the biological and chemical giant Ciba in the wake of its expansion into mainland China in the 1990s. By the end of 1995, at the point where it merged with former competitor Sandoz, the corporation's operations had expanded to the point where Ciba-Geigy (China) Ltd, the umbrella operation in China, was providing the focal point for about 13 joint ventures, cooperative agreements, and wholly owned companies.

Earlier in the decade the company had been engaged in a systematic campaign in its European home territories to change the culture of the organization from being hierarchical and paternalistic to having a work style based on ''directed autonomy and empowerment,'' leadership and teamwork.

Now it wanted to extend this culture to its worldwide network of joint ventures and subsidiaries. To this end, it embarked on an intensive program of training for its technical and professional staff, coordinated and delivered at a regional level, to develop their leadership, team-building, and coaching skills so that each individual could provide the necessary support and advice for staff under their supervision.

Joan Lewis, HR Director for Ciba's China and Hong Kong operations for over five years and now a successful consultant on management issues in China, stresses what this entailed in a part of the world with complex cross-cultural undercurrents:

''Among mainland Chinese there is still an inherent and understandable respect for elders and thus for senior managers who are regarded as mentors. However, 'directed empowerment' means that in certain circumstances you have to be able to question your immediate superior on key issues and suggest alternative ways of undertaking tasks. Because the majority of front-line workers are relatively unskilled, and because responsibility comes very early, there is enormous pressure to provide training at the most basic level, not only telling staff how they should undertake essential tasks but also explaining 'why?'"

A similar process was underway at the same time in another Asia-based international, the high-tech manufacturer Texas Instruments. Texas Instruments had been in Asia for about 30 years but had traditionally used the region as a base for manufacturing goods for export to North America and Europe. But in the late 1980s, Asian demand for the company's products shot up and the firm was forced to change this stance.

Not only were the company's new customers local to the region, but they also demanded products that were integrated with their own technological systems. "We were not geared up for this," admitted the company's then president for Asia, Marco Landi. "In Taiwan, for example, we were one of the largest manufacturers of semiconductor products, yet we had only 1% of the country's domestic market."

To shift attitudes in the company to the point where it took the needs of local customers seriously, Landi overhauled its approach to quality. Previously Texas Instruments had followed a "zero defect" strategy. Now the emphasis was shifted to improving customer satisfaction and achieving "preferred" supplier status.

At the heart of the new strategy was the creation of new work teams that managed themselves: planning, controlling, and improving their own work processes, setting their own goals, and inspecting their own work. This, clearly, had implications for the way supervisors and line managers influenced performance and productivity.

To help in the shift from a hierarchical management style to one based on teamwork and decision by consensus, Texas Instruments invested in attitude training to enable managers and supervisors throughout Asia to get to know each other better and create an environment in which everyone felt able to operate effectively. This approach has also been adopted by Asia-based employers in a variety of other sectors.

At Hong Kong's Hang Seng Bank, for example, vice-chairman Alexander Au has spearheaded two-way communications with front-line staff to ensure they are able to provide a better service to the bank's customers.

"We began to hold regular communications training sessions to explain Bank policies clearly and concisely," he says. "Our staff are often the first point of contact with customers and it is essential that they can respond quickly and explain our messages. This means that they should always be clear about our policies and services, while we in turn can learn about our customers' needs from them."

Similarly, Holiday Inn, which has expanded rapidly into mainland China, provided its locally recruited staff at the company's new Crown Plaza Hotel in Chengdu with three months of intensive training before the opening. "The main challenge was giving them the confidence to deal with complaints and requests effectively," says general manager Michael Bastiaanse.

St Charles pilgrimage

The second strategy adopted by global corporations is to place technical and professional staff recruited anywhere in the world through common foundation training in a home-based, in-company center. The goal here is two-fold. In terms of global corporate strategy it ensures that services or products are delivered to a consistent standard. The assumption is that the core clientele for a global company are other global companies who will expect the same service in Singapore or Moscow that they receive in, say, New York or Paris.

The other aim is to provide new entrants with a common technical foundation and, equally importantly, an internal professional network that will ensure that they can be transferred anywhere in the firm's global diaspora, and adapt quickly and without personal career disruption.

The best example of this approach is the training provided to all its graduate recruits by the former accountancy giant Arthur Andersen and its sister consultancy practice. Throughout Arthur Andersen's global expansion in the 1980s and 1990s, it relied almost exclusively on newly recruited graduates from universities around the world rather than, as in other practices, experienced staff with at least three years of post-qualification work behind them.

It was able to do this because of the level of investment it placed in its foundation training, which even as early as 1987 was costing it in excess of $80mn a year and by the turn of the century was topping $200mn. This was a mix of technical design and implementation (which underpinned the firm's core expertise in IT systems work) and business acumen (which enabled its staff to link information technology solutions to the client's strategic needs, and to do so anywhere in the world).

A certain proportion of this training took place in the firm's regional centers. In Europe, for example, regional training facilities were located at its offices in London, Segovia, and Geneva. The basic "core" training, however, was conducted at the firm's international training center at St Charles, some 45 miles outside Chicago.

This extraordinary firm-specific campus is as large as those of many world-class universities. At its peak, in the mid-1990s, the center ran 1500 courses and accommodated 50,000 students every year. Two conference centers, two amphitheaters, a 5574-square-meter (60,000-square-foot) Education Development Building, 500 computer work stations, and an extensive sports center and clubhouse rendered the St Charles visit made by trainees from Europe, Canada, Latin America, the Middle East, South Asia, and Asia-Pacific a common formative experience, which shaped their thinking about the company for the rest of their careers. It was quite common for students on the same course – the firm adopted the same "cadre" system used by universities – to meet again at the stages in their careers when they returned to St Charles to continue their professional education.

The highly centralized nature of the training always had to be tempered by project-based training to allow newly qualified graduates to test theory against practice. This has been particularly true in China, where the size, structure, and rapid growth of companies was not typical of those encountered by Andersen in other parts of the world.

The range of projects at the Greater China practice was greater than almost anywhere else in the world. In Hong Kong this included designing and implementing a project at the Hong Kong Stock Exchange, which resulted in paperless training; in Shanghai it included helping a motorcycle manufacturer establish a new management system, refine its management procedures, and train its staff. "Because of the variety of assignments I never have the feeling I am repeating the same work," a third-year consultant recruited from Jiaotong University commented in the late 1990s. "Every day, I try something new and learn something new."

THE TRANSNATIONAL COMPANY MODEL: KNOWLEDGE EXCHANGE AND BOTTOM-UP INNOVATION

As Chapter 4 described, the danger of a top-down transfer of technology and knowledge is that it leaves the center unaware of local conditions and opportunities that might warrant adapting core strategies or business processes. The essence of "think global, act local," as stressed by the University of Michigan's Dave Ulrich (profiled in Chapter 8), is the bottom-up and side-to-side exchange of information and new ideas. This is especially important in loosely federated groups of subsidiaries or where companies have opted for commercial alliances rather than merger or acquisition.

As a result, global training and development initiatives in transnational companies often form part of larger organizational strategies. The purpose here is not just the transfer and inculcation of key company technology or knowledge but the capture of experiences and insights, and their use, to create new firm-specific concepts or ideas.

This is most widely practiced during senior management courses and board-level education initiatives. Grand Metropolitan, the worldwide food company that is now a part of the Diageo Group, launched a group-wide effort to increase its presence in emerging markets as part of the growth strategy introduced by its newly appointed chief executive, George Bull, in 1993.

A survey by the company's group HR department revealed that GrandMet subsidiaries had already drawn up plans for commercial expansion into countries like Russia, China, and India. However, it also revealed that senior managers in these subsidiaries had widely differing levels of experience and knowledge of these countries. Some had little or no knowledge or direct experience; others had a lifetime of working knowledge. The disparity was worsened by the competition that existed between subsidiaries, which resulted in little or no information being exchanged about lessons learned or data acquired. In one case, two different subsidiaries had commissioned research on commercial conditions in Asia from the same US consultancy, and jealously guarded the same conclusions from each other.

A series of briefings was organized for the 60 top managers across all GrandMet subsidiaries. Designed to focus participants' attention on the practical implications of the corporation's plans to expand its commercial presence in mainland China, the briefings were structured around one-hour sessions that allowed speakers to make their own formal input and then to participate in a facilitated discussion, which enabled the group to draw on the good practice and commercial knowledge of the more experienced members. Considerable care was taken to choose subjects that were of direct interest to participants, and to match these with input from senior executives having direct practical knowledge in the chosen field.

Accordingly, the speakers included the general manager for business development for Courtaulds, who discussed the intricacies of joint-venture negotiations; the director of human resources for Ciba-Geigy (China), who discussed the HR implications of commercial expansion on the mainland; and the former business development manager for Coca-Cola China, who discussed the problems of distribution. A video interview with Shell's director for Central China, commissioned especially for the event, provided the focus for discussions on marketing and branding. At a formal dinner on the evening before the event, the group was addressed by the executive director of Wheelock & Co., one of the four top trading houses in Asia, on the future role of Hong Kong.

The group consisted of the top marketing, finance, brand, and HR directors of flagship companies like Burger King, Smirnoff, Häagen-Dazs, Pillsbury, and J&B. Many had never had the opportunity to share their experiences with counterparts in other countries, and the capacity of the briefing to foster corporate-wide organizational learning was reinforced immeasurably as a result. The added bonus was a group-wide taskforce formed to coordinate the corporate effort in China, making it more effective while saving on costs.

Trust as a surrogate for structure

The cardinal need for organizational learning can also be built into training and development initiatives at other levels of the organization. Lufthansa is one of the founding members of the Star Alliance that now includes United Airlines, Air Canada, Varig (of Brazil), Scandinavian Airlines (SAS), and Thai Airlines among others. As such, it does not face the difficulty of creating common standards of customer service and quality across different subsidiaries of the same corporation but rather across different companies over which it has no direct control.

"The key question for us is how we create a common sense of identity and purpose between flight attendants in Chicago, purchasing agents in India and maintenance staff in Beijing," says Thomas Sattelberger, Lufthansa's director of human resources. "In a situation where old fashioned management authority is not present, we have to draw on other means. Above all, we have to recognize that trust is becoming a surrogate for structure."

In the late 1990s, Lufthansa worked with other members of the Star Alliance to design a series of joint initiatives that would help achieve this. These varied from setting up joint venues where employees from the different companies could "meet, eat and greet" to help managers and their staff develop an awareness of each other; organizing inter-company roadshows to help staff at all levels to gain a common understanding of the aims and objectives of the Star Alliance; running combined training and development programs and cross-cultural work-shops to provide essential project management, interpersonal, and team-working skills in the context of the new cross-boundary organiza-tion; and setting up young manager and technician exchanges to build a new cadre of professional staff used to developing new problem-solving approaches across the whole alliance.

At the top of the organization, the Star partners set up eight core working groups in 1996 to explore different aspects such as the route network, product harmonization, and station services. The chairman of each of these groups reported to an alliance development committee in which two members of each airline were charged with implementing the partnership strategy authorized by an alliance development board, which in turn consisted of one director from each airline.

The arrangement is similar to those adopted by other airline alliances, but hard experience shows that the formal structure is less important than the level of cooperation between the partners. "It's still a major issue to get the alliance mentality over to several thousand managers," says Sattelberger. "The people in the front line are the decisive factor – how the station managers from different airlines in Rio get along together. The degree to which people exchange knowledge is directly correlated to the give and take attitude and thrust of the partners."

CONCLUSION: STRIPPING AWAY THE EMPEROR'S CLOTHES

This chapter has focused largely on the strategies and aims underpinning global training and development initiatives, and how these are closely linked to the various stages of global commercial activity identified by Sumantra Ghoshal and Christopher Bartlett. It has not focused in detail on the techniques and methodology of delivering these programs because they are no different to those in domestically oriented initiatives, described in other ExpressExec guides such as *Management Development*, *E-Training and Development*, *Developing the Individual*, and *Boardroom Education*.

There tends to be a false mystique about any global business initiative. The HR practitioner, program designer, external consultant and academic, and participants all tend to talk up the experience because it glorifies their status. The glamor is boosted still further by the fact that most global training and development activities take place in exotic locations and entail sophisticated human interchanges, even where this is not a core part of the curriculum.

Yet strip away the glamor and there is little difference from what takes place domestically. A research project by Jo Howard of the UK's Roffey Park Management Institute in 1990 found that managers in inner-city branches of banks, stores, and other high-street enterprises often have to manage similar cross-cultural tasks as their counterparts in overseas subsidiaries, and require the same lateral-mindedness, sensitivity to other cultures, and willingness to experiment with new ideas.

The purpose of global development activities is also similar – to break down barriers, promote cross-functional team-working, and foster trust between people with different perspectives. The "Spearhead China" initiative at GrandMet was important not just because it helped to make top executives aware of the differences in culture between themselves and their Chinese counterparts, but because it made them aware of the differences in culture between people of the same race in different subsidiaries.

The need for two-way communication is critical. Program designers and tutors need to listen and learn from the feedback they receive from participants, as well as impart their expert knowledge. It is also critical that any initiative is designed in collaboration with people who understand the region under focus and that, given the complexity of the issues that are often involved, tutors work with members of the relevant product and service groups in the organization, who can often play important roles in helping to design and implement the program.

KEY LEARNING POINTS

» Companies at various stages of their entry into international markets have contrasting global training needs.
» Companies that still consist of loosely federated subsidiaries or self-sustaining local operations confine their focus to the selection and development, usually at an early stage of their careers, of a pool of general managers who can run these operations at a distance. This is usually achieved by conventional fast-track schemes (see ExpressExec guide on *Management Development*) adapted to include challenging projects in a number of key overseas locations.
» Companies with highly integrated manufacturing processes or service standards place more emphasis on centrally designed company-wide training that transfers technology and quality standards consistently across their global network. These are either delivered locally to centrally imposed standards or at regional or global training centers.
» Companies with transnational goals of thinking globally but acting locally place a premium on initiatives that not only transfer centrally determined concepts and quality standards but allow a two-way exchange of knowledge, experience, and

good practice. This is also the case between members of joint-venture or strategic alliances, where sharing technology and market acumen is a key incentive to take part.
» These imperatives are not mutually exclusive. Some organizations, like Shell (see Chapter 5), pursue fast-track management development schemes, top-down technology transfer, and two-way knowledge exchange schemes simultaneously, according to need.

FURTHER READING

Ghoshal, S. & Bartlett, C.A. (1989) *Managing across Borders: The transnational solution*. Harvard Business School Press, Boston.

Ghoshal, S. & Bartlett, C.A. (1998) *The Individualized Corporation: A fundamentally new approach to management*. Heinemann, London.

Redding, G. & Armitage, C. (1993) *Management Development in Asia-Pacific*. Economist Intelligence Unit, Hong Kong.

Syrett, M. (1994) "Questions of quality." *Asian Business*, March.

Syrett, M. (1995) "Finders, keepers: strategies of hanging onto your best employees." *Asia-Pacific HR Monitor*, summer.

Syrett, M. (1998) "A new cultural environment: what's it like to work for a multinational?" *China Casebook*.

Syrett, M. & Lammiman, J. (1998) "Lean companies get fit." *MBA: The magazine for business masters*, January.

In Practice

» BMW: Inception and first steps
» Volkswagen/Skoda: Early partnership teething problems
» Banco Bilbao Vizcaya: Knowledge transfer in a service sector
» Lufthansa: Transformation through alliance

The last chapter stressed that "global" companies enter international markets in contrasting states of readiness and that the level of transformation they have to undergo, largely achieved through training and development initiatives, reflects their prior domestic strategies.

In other words, going global is a by-product of a domestically determined growth strategy, not the other way around. Unless a company concerned is extraordinarily forward-looking, the way it conducts business abroad will be much the same as the way it conducted it at home. What follows is a very rapid and painful learning curve, as senior executives quickly discover that what they understand by performance management, productivity, empowerment, quality management, and leadership may not be the same as what local staff, supervisors, and executives understand by the terms. At this point, if the chief executive has any sense, global training turns from a top-down exercise into a two-way exchange – and everyone starts to realize that globalization is a journey that does not end once the initial goals have been achieved.

The examples in this chapter try to illustrate the point. For example, the BMW case focuses on the early formative period of the company's international strategy, while the Volkswagen/Skoda and Banco Bilbao Vizcaya cases cover the intermediate period once the company had made the decision and chosen an international partner. The Lufthansa case, by contrast, covers the most recent period in the company's journey, building on the early stages of its relationship with the Star Alliance, described in Chapter 6.

BMW: INCEPTION AND FIRST STEPS

When people discuss global management development, they usually have the needs of a company like BMW in mind. Yet the transition from a national to a global company has been remarkably recent. In the last decade BMW has moved very rapidly from being – in its own words – a Bavarian-based and German-thinking car manufacturer to being a global player in its industry through a combination of organic growth, acquisitions, and local joint ventures.

The key events in its recent history include:

» the opening of a manufacturing plant in Spartanburg, South Carolina, in 1993;
» the purchase of the UK Rover Group in 1994, which has led to a number of joint ventures;
» the establishment of new subsidiaries in emerging markets such as Brazil, South China, and South Korea;
» an engine plant jointly built with Chrysler, and launched in 1996, in Latin America;
» a return to Formula One racing after 15 years' absence, as part of a number of measures recently taken to strengthen the BMW brand.

For Klaus Bodel, BMW's head of international management development, "German thinking" gave him the most cause for thought during this period. "At the start of the journey we are still making, many managers in BMW still perceived the marketplace as traditionally European. Very quickly, we were put into a situation where we had to reposition the brand in a variety of different markets, from East Asia where people have chauffeurs and luxury still rules, to those in Europe where environmental issues and energy conservation take precedent."

This meant, almost self-evidently, that BMW's German managers needed to develop a global perspective and the sensitivity to work effectively with counterparts from their overseas partners and subsidiaries. The acquisition of Rover in 1994 was a good case in point, according to Bodel. "All the British tabloid newspapers dug up analogies of the Battle of Britain and German tanks rolling over British lawns. For the first time German engineers had to work directly with British engineers. We had to organize meetings in Brussels to foster mutual understanding and to clarify how we were going to play the game."

The company's entry into emerging markets presented further international development challenges. For the first time, BMW appointed managers from local countries to key control posts. Not only did German managers have to travel overseas to work with their counterparts at the sites of subsidiary plants, but local managers also needed to visit the company headquarters in Munich to learn about the mindset and methods of German engineers.

To overcome the barriers to cross-cultural working of this kind, Bodel designed a systematic development program that involved:

» international management training;
» cross-national corporate training (for example, a popular module entitled "BMW International");
» cross-national task forces on specific issues such as purchasing and procurement, and auditing procedures;
» cross-functional assignments for high-potential managers; and
» a new international trainee program.

This program was based on a new philosophy that a cross-cultural mindset is necessary for any managerial post, regardless of whether it is formally designated as international. "In every workshop and program we ran, we wanted to leave delegates with the message that prejudice is a barrier to your competence as a manager," Bodel stresses. "If you choose to participate in the event as part of your personal development you will receive all the help you need in the form of coaching, mentoring, and support from the HR function. If you do not, we will assess you very critically because without this preparation we do not think you will be very effective in your post."

Creating a genuinely cross-cultural culture, Bodel emphasizes, is a journey rather than a destination. Not all of the local managers of the subsidiaries signed up to the process overnight. "From the launch of our Spartanburg venture, we wanted to encourage an exchange of visits of German and US managers in order to foster a mutual understanding of the culture on both sides. Despite the high priority we placed on this, it took us over two years to convince the management staff that it was in their interest to undertake this kind of intercultural training."

In Germany, Bodel had to work hard to rid overseas assignments of the stigma of failure they traditionally carried. "Until 1991, those managers that wanted to get rid of their low performers sent them abroad," he says. "We had created an atmosphere where going abroad seemed to suggest that you either had no other jobs available to you in your own department, or that you were perceived as unsuccessful or a failure.

"Now people are given a personal career plan and are provided with support throughout each assignment, including the challenge of integrating into the parent organization at the end of the assignment. Fostering an international spirit is no longer a question of an individual's willingness, bur rather his or her readiness in terms of language skills, professional skills, and the potential to be developed."

BMW's first steps towards a global market strategy illustrate that, contrary to the retrospective gloss many organizations paint on their own achievements, there is no clear road; instead there is more of an emergent sense of purpose governing the task. Even as late as 1997, the company was still asking itself the following "open" questions.

1 Should we develop international, or just multinational, management at BMW?
2 If international management is required, will it comprise managerial staff with international skills "across the board" or just a few "global" managers?
3 The global market is having a tremendous impact on manufacturing, marketing, and service – what kind of changes will be necessary?

KEY INSIGHTS

» "Globalization is a journey. There is no end point." (Klaus Bodel)
» It usually involves extensive training at all levels.

VOLKSWAGEN/SKODA: EARLY PARTNERSHIP TEETHING TROUBLES

Most early global steps have been made by acquiring the right knowledge and local capability through an acquisition, joint venture, or commercial alliance. At this point the cross-cultural dynamics identified by Geert Hofstede (see Chapter 8) start kicking in big time, with training as the main solution.

Volkswagen (VW) put training and development at the heart of its efforts to forge a viable alliance with its Czech counterpart Skoda. At the time the joint venture was launched in April 1991, Skoda was regarded as a sick joke by many Western car manufacturers; but as Skoda's Biagio Morabito affirms, in the eyes of its managers and by the (flawed) standards of the region, Skoda was one of the top producers of Central and Eastern Europe and a company they were proud to work for.

"Before the revolution of 1989, Skoda was an exemplary state enterprise," he claims. "All the main decisions of the enterprise were subject to state planning. Quantitative achievement of planned figures took absolute priority over entrepreneurial decisions. The organization of the company corresponded to socialist structure, being centralistic and autocratic.

"Accordingly, management composed of a director and his seven deputies was strictly hierarchical. Purchasing and selling prices were not subject to the laws of offer and demand, but were controlled by government. In addition, investment and production volumes were subject to state planning. However, Skoda was able to organize its production and work processes itself. A great production depth and high level of supplies were designed to make the enterprise independent."

Looking back in the light of what he knows now about the West's production techniques, Morabito regarded Skoda, compared with other Central and Eastern European automobile manufacturers, as "the one-eyed king in the country of the blind"; by regional standards a good company, which was nonetheless incapable of withstanding international competition.

In these circumstances Skoda, as a potential partner for a Western car manufacturer, offered a number of strengths and weaknesses. The morale of its managers and workers was high. In its own eyes, Skoda, one of the oldest automobile manufacturers in Europe, had a long tradition of success in its established markets like Poland and the countries of the former Soviet Union, and was a trademark to be proud of. It still had the pioneering spirit that, once again in its own eyes, had developed creative and original solutions to bypass the constraints of a politically motivated command economy. And, in common with most other Central and Eastern European enterprises, it had a well-qualified workforce in engineering and quantitative management techniques, although little or no understanding of customer service and market research.

The challenge for VW was to introduce new production techniques that would make the company capable of competing in new international markets without undermining the sense of pride that Skoda's managers and workers had in their company. At a time when leading German car firms like BMW and VW were themselves facing increasing pressure from Japanese and US competition, this was no easy task.

As Peter Kunz, the human resources director responsible for designing the process of learning, explains: "Volkswagen was passing through its own change process. Our technical knowledge was high but our ability to respond to change has been slower. We therefore felt that simply introducing our own proven methods of the past would not be enough. Skoda would be lagging behind VW and would be one step behind us and could never arrive at an international competitor's level.

"In addition, a direct carry-over of knowledge would have totally ignored the origin and present-day state of Skoda in the Czech Republic, and would even have ignored or destroyed the fruitful starting points of the past. Possibly, considerable passive resistance of the local workers defending their own cultural identity would result."

The solution VW came up with was a strategy of "know-how transfer" that would enable Skoda managers to link their own traditions with modern VW approaches to international competition. The strategy took the form of a four-part process.

1 At the start of the joint venture, managers from the VW group were appointed to key positions at Skoda such as sales, production control, and quality management. Through these managers, the basic strategy of Skoda was agreed with the VW group management.

2 Other principal functions were filled, on a shared basis, by a local Skoda manager and a VW expatriate. The German manager acted as a "buddy," teaching and coaching the Czech manager. As the local manager gained confidence and increasingly took on responsibility, the expatriate drew back from operative and strategic tasks, and concentrated solely on coaching. As Peter Kunz explains, the demands on the coach were high. "If their social ability is insufficient there is a danger that his or her Czech colleague will become incapable of taking action due to a state of insecurity, and will take

on the role of a mere assistant to the German partner – not our intention at all.''

3 Counselors and specialists supported the Czech colleague on site for a period of up to one year in fields of activity where up-to-date specific know-how was lacking.

4 In some fields, for example personnel management, the transfer of know-how took place through project management. The Czech manager in this case was the only holder of the function and was thus secure in his status and activity. Together with German counterparts in VW, these Czech managers defined a series of projects directly linked to the joint-venture strategy in which they were to cooperate and of which, in the course of time, they were to take control.

As Kunz stresses, the demands this placed on the German manager-buddies, acting as coaches and tutors, was immense. VW has built up a series of competences that they regard as essential if know-how is to be transferred to Skoda managers successfully. These include:

» *intercultural sensitivity and open-mindedness*, having the readiness to live in the Czech Republic and to try to understand the country and the people;

» *leadership and the ability to change roles*, in particular the ability to change over between a patriarchal and a partner-like style of management depending on the situation, and the readiness and confidence to ''let go'' and make oneself superfluous;

» *process competence*, having the ability to identify the most important tasks in an organizational unit, convert these to processes with measurable results, and place them in a strategic and forward-looking context;

» *the ability of analysis and learning*, asking the right questions and purposefully linking usable aspects of the local environment with one's own know-how; and

» *standing*, having the ability to link the positive aspects of the two corporate cultures – that of the Czech environment and one's own original VW culture – and reflect these in one's actions towards both sides in a self-confident manner.

These competences were developed as a result of hard experience. Peter Kunz has listed ten major mistakes initially made by German and Czech managers in the course of know-how transfer:

1 wrong choice of personnel on both sides – for example, specialists selected instead of experienced managers;
2 no individual preparation for the role of know-how donor and acceptor;
3 the two parties only try to deal with the solution of production problems, not with the process of learning;
4 the German manager feels responsible for strategy development and reports to VW group management, leaving the Czech manager with only operative tasks;
5 no systematic and rapid process of informing staff about all the principal changes – in critical situations the Germans only talk to Germans;
6 the expatriate is concerned with his profile and status, while the Czech managers appear satisfied with the role of "assistant";
7 the expatriate fails to set up a list of the existing processes that work but immediately questions everything, pushing through his own concepts and, as a result, "deskilling" the Czech managers;
8 the entire organization is too task-oriented, with little attempt made to gain cooperation through team-building and regular briefings with Czech managers;
9 no unambiguous agreements as to strategic and management targets; and
10 no joint self-critical reflection as to milestones in the development of the new organizational unit.

However, Skoda's Biagio Morabito is a firm believer in the theories of "double-loop" learning pioneered by Harvard Business School's Professor Chris Argyris (see ExpressExec guide *Management Development*), in which curiosity is followed by disillusionment, which in turns leads to perseverance and ultimately success.

"With Volkswagen support, Skoda is entering the New Age in large steps," he concludes. "After initial euphoria, a phase of sobriety has set in. The process of change is more complicated and lengthy than was originally expected. At present, at a time that is also characterized by difficult overall economic conditions, the main point is to follow up on the fruitful beginnings we created in the first five years consistently and unremittingly. If this is done, success will be certain for us.''

KEY INSIGHTS

» Globalization usually involves extensive training at all levels.
» Intercultural sensitivity and open-mindedness; leadership and the ability to change roles; process competence; the ability of analysis and learning; and, above all, standing – the ability to link the positive aspects of the corporate cultures of all partners and reflect these in practice – are essential parts of the curriculum.
» Key managers should be concerned with the transfer of learning, not just production and process issues. Local managers should feel part of the strategic process and not be left with purely operative roles.

BANCO BILBAO Y VISCAYA: KNOWLEDGE TRANSFER IN A SERVICE SECTOR

While VW was struggling with the post-communist agenda of its chosen partner in the Czech republic, the Spanish bank Banco Bilbao y Viscaya (BBV) was encountering similar problems with a portfolio of partners in Latin America.

Latin America was obvious territory for newly ascendant Spanish firms. By 1998, BBV had invested some 2bn pesetas in acquisitions in Venezuela, Colombia, Peru, Puerto Rico, Argentina, and Panama – giving them, in the process, control over 1500 branch offices and 1100 automatic cash dispensers, numbers that have since doubled.

BBV's strategy was to obtain market entrance into each Latin American country by buying into a local bank and signing a management agreement with other shareholders. It does not favor setting up greenfield operations, believing this approach would be too costly and take too long to achieve results.

"We were particularly interested in Latin America because of the region's high development potential,'' explains José Ignacio Goirigol zarri Tellaeche, the BBV general manager with overall responsibility for the region. "Its cultural, historic, and linguistic links with Spain and Spanish ways of doing business were also significant attractions."

But, as with BMW's acquisition of Rover and VW's partnership with Skoda, buying into a market through a firm with a local presence brings its own problems. Many of the banks in Latin America are family-owned and conservative in their business philosophy. Local boardroom and senior management traditions did not fit in well with BBV's ethic of rapid expansion and its development of competitive products that would improve the speed and quality of their banking operations.

"The need to train managers for Latin America faced us with a big new challenge," says José Luiz Carranza Ortíz, BBV general manager with overall responsibility for HR. "We tackled this at the outset by sending out small but critical teams of five or six managers who could help us 'export' the BBV model of banking. This was particularly important in the area of retail banking which is one of our key strengths."

In addition, BBV assembled a Latin American support group of about 100 experts, in areas such as IT, marketing, human resources, retail banking, financial market operations, and private banking, that newly acquired subsidiaries could use as a resource – but the traffic was not just one-way.

"We then brought over to Spain key local top managers for our future Latin American operations. They spent two to three years working for BBV in Spain, and we also arranged for them to bring their families over with them," says Carranza. "This was a very large exercise and one that was difficult to organize, but it was essential in order to give the managers concerned the necessary feel for the BBV way of doing things."

The expatriate program affected 100 Latin American managers, and the families and the executive concerned were mainly from upper-middle and senior management levels. "We also undertook a number of multi-country training courses," Carranza concludes. "These included a one-week course in Mexico for both Spanish and Latin American managers, and a two-week course in risk management."

LUFTHANSA: TRANSFORMATION THROUGH ALLIANCE

The examples so far have one thing in common. Different training methods may have been employed, but they were all in response to a strategy of international growth by acquisition and turnaround. BMW, VW, and BBV all gained entry to new markets by acquiring ailing local companies that nonetheless offered a vital presence, local brand equity, and market intelligence.

However acquisition has not been the only route forward. Joint ventures had always been an alternative, particularly for companies wishing to expand into mainland China. In the 1990s, the principle behind joint-venturing was expanded into full-blown commercial alliances – and nowhere has it proved more popular than in the airline industry.

Alliance growth in air transport was initially prompted by deregulation in the US and by the slow increase in competition round the world as the process of privatizing national airlines got under way in the 1980s. But by the mid-1990s, liberalization still had a long way to go. The majority of international airlines were state-controlled, if not state-owned, and Byzantine regulations protected their freedom of maneuver. Then, as now, European airlines could not normally fly between destinations in the US, and US carriers were similarly constrained in Europe. But however slow and laborious the negotiations, controls were being reduced and the airlines were becoming increasingly worried about their ability to compete and survive.

One such was Lufthansa, German's state-owned airline. In 1997 Frank Reid, the company's president and chief executive commented: "We are being hammered by the same market forces that are putting pressure on the whole industry. Airport charges, already too high, are rising by a further 24 percent. Space is at a premium and despite strenuous efforts on our part, we are only receiving 75 percent of the revenue from each ticket we sell."

In the circumstances, Reid was more than happy to take a leading role in setting up the Star Alliance in 1995, consisting of his own company and United Airlines, Air Canada, Varig (of Brazil), Scandinavian Airlines (SAS), and Thai Airlines among others. Star is easily the largest alliance in terms of the number of companies involved. Unusually, there is no central authority. In terms of "soft" issues like customer service and relationship marketing, the strength of the network depends on its weakest link. There is no obvious mechanism for the stronger members like Lufthansa to exert pressure on the weaker airlines. Any improvement has to be achieved through sharing experience and best practice.

Drawing on this experience, as described in more detail in Chapter 6, HR director Thomas Sattelberger drew up a series of programs and events designed not only to instil an alliance mentality among staff from different members of the Star conglomerate but to encourage them to share their knowledge and experience. These included international roadshows to communicate the ideas and vision of the alliance, and cross-cultural workshops and management development programs designed specifically to encourage executives from all member companies to work together in coming up with new strategies for the alliance.

However the initial phase of the Star Alliance training strategy was only the tip of the iceberg. Lufthansa's entry to global markets through the alliance triggered and was fueled by its own internal transformation from an old-fashioned corporate monolith to a networked company where key functions were outsourced or performed by staff with whom Lufthansa did not have a direct employer–employee relationship.

The company had gained valuable experience in "borderless learning" in the early 1990s when the company outsourced support functions such as check-in services, aircraft maintenance, and food service. Surveys indicate that these services account for up to 66 percent of customers' stated flight satisfaction. So managers at Lufthansa had to provide what Sattelberger calls "network glue": designing seamless transnational structures to develop a global outlook in all staff and inspire the right level of customer service from the "absent ones" (staff not employed by Lufthansa but who perform important tasks on the company's behalf).

By the time it took the decision to help found the Star Alliance, Lufthansa had already developed a model of strategy and management that was heavily stakeholder-biased. In its own right, it employed 90,000 people. Through the alliance, it was a leading force in transforming technology and good practice to 15 other airlines whose network now spans 800 destinations in over 130 countries of the world.

"The key question for us is how we create a common sense of identity and purpose between flight attendants in Chicago, purchasing agents in India, and maintenance staff in Beijing," Sattelberger commented in 1997. "In a situation where old-fashioned management authority is not present, we have to draw on other means. Above all, we have to recognize that trust is becoming a surrogate for structure."

To achieve the twin aims of internal and allied people development, Lufthansa took a leaf out of the books of large US corporations and founded one of Europe's first corporate universities in the spring of 1998. The model the company clearly had in mind was the John F. Welch Leadership Center, General Electric's own university at Crotonville in New York State, as the excerpts from the mission statements of the two institutes illustrate (Table 7.1).

All of the programs of the Lufthansa School of Business are built on a common model, called the "Lufthansa Leadership Compass," which describes the key requirements that the company places now and in the future on both its executives and its entire staff in order to meet the strategic goals of the Star Alliance. These include:

» motivating others;
» breakthrough problem-solving;
» people leadership;
» entrepreneurial leadership;
» attitude and drive; and, above all,
» a passion for business.

As with GE's Crotonville center, the Lufthansa School works with a number of academic partners. Drawing on existing relationships forged

Table 7.1 A comparison of the corporate universities of GE and Lufthansa in terms of their statedmissions.

John F. Welch Leadership Center	Lufthansa School of Business
Help GE managers grow and develop through education and training	Support the strategic direction of the group effectively
Transfer best practice, corporate initiatives, and change management concepts	Keep "intellectual capital" as an essential part of the company and as a means of development
Partner with the business to educate, develop, and build with their customers and external constituencies	Link both the academic expertise and the experience of partner companies to the business practices of Lufthansa
Be a conduit for transmitting GE's culture and values	Offer opportunities and steps for individual personal development, while stimulating and driving a shared management and performance culture

by other companies in the Star Alliance, the school has links with the Cranfield School of Management and London Business School in the UK, INSEAD in France, Canada's McGill University, and the Indian Institute of Management in Bangalore.

Among the many courses to emerge from this exceptionally rich mix is the "*Steigflug*/Climb" program. Designed for a group of 160 executives working in or with Star Alliance partners, this modular course runs parallel to the job and lasts one year. Major seminars with all participants create a common "task undertaking." This is tested and expanded by breaking the cadre into small groups of five to eight managers, and analyzing the quality of Lufthansa's leadership and performance culture through a worldwide benchmarking exercise that encompasses not only other partner companies in the alliance but major international competitors.

To sustain their work, and that of staff on other courses, the Lufthansa School has established a series of intranet-based training and information centers using a dedicated software program, "Lufthansa Learnway." These are available to all employees to support both study on Lufthansa School courses and their own self-directed learning.

Through this medium, the company has developed a series of firm-specific change management techniques that have helped Lufthansa front-line managers broaden their links with Star Alliance staff. A good example is "the Armada" model of rapid communication, developed by Thomas Sattelberger and the manager of the Lufthansa School, Michael Heuser, which helps executives reach a critical mass of employees quickly by means of:

» many high-speed events ("speedboats");
» a few large events ("ocean liners"); or
» a mixture of the two ("the Armada").

Newly promoted to the board of Lufthansa as executive vice-president for products and services, Sattelberger is now responsible for the rapid development of product management, ground services, customer services, the expansion of airport terminal facilities, and cabin-crew services.

For him the whole process comes down to one word – trust. "In the end, achieving sustainable market share in what are now global markets comes down to creating good relationships. In an age when conventional employer–employee relationships are breaking down, this will only work if people feel there is integrity and authenticity in what the company is saying to them. In a virtual world, trust has become the surrogate for structure."

KEY INSIGHTS

» The transfer of knowledge and good practice between partners is a key incentive for taking part in a strategic alliance. This is invariably the task of the global training and development function.
» "When conventional barriers between partners no longer exist, trust is the surrogate for structure." (Thomas Sattelberger)

Key Concepts and Thinkers

The ideas underpinning the design and delivery of global training and development initiatives cover anything from cross-cultural theory to new distance-learning technology. We have also included new thinking on what globalism actually is, as this often defines the parameters of new initiatives.

This is the one field of training and development where the chief executive is actively engaged. As a consequence, the list of influential thinkers includes a higher than average proportion of present or former industrial captains, including the former CEO of ICI John Harvey-Jones; Percy Barnevik of Asea Brown Boveri, the originator of the famous philosophy ''think global, act local;'' and the god-like figure of GE's Jack Welch, the creator of the ''boundaryless'' organization.

CROSS-CULTURAL MANAGEMENT

This essential skill of global trading was first explored systematically in the 1970s, when the management of local staff and collaboration with local suppliers and customers started to be conducted on an equal basis (see Chapter 3).

The father figure of cross-cultural management is **Geert Hofstede**, a Dutch engineer who switched to studying psychology in the 1960s. Originally a foreman and plant manager at IBM in Holland, he became the corporation's chief psychologist. The post gave him unparalleled access to the different nationalities working for IBM, and through a series of diagnostic interviews – later expanded to encompass staff of other multinationals when he took up academic research work at international schools like INSEAD and IMD – he was able to identify four dimensions governing cultural diversity. These are:

1 *Uncertainty avoidance*: this refers to how comfortable, or threatened, people feel about ambiguity and the unknown. Individuals in the latter group often have a marked preference for formal rules and strict definitions of right and wrong.
2 *Power distance*: defined by Hofstede as ''the extent to which the less powerful members of institutions and organizations accept that power is distributed unequally.''
3 *Masculinity – femininity*: masculine cultures tend to have very marked expectations of gender roles in society while feminine

cultures show a greater fluidity. In "feminine" cultures such as the Nordic countries and in the Netherlands, Hofstede argues "soft" management skills are practiced just as much by men as by women.

4 *Individualism – collectivism*: the extent to which a society favors individual over collective action and effort. The more affluent a country becomes, Hofstede finds, the more it moves towards individualism. The US has a notably individualist culture, for example, in contrast to Latin American countries.

In 1980 Hofstede co-founded the Institute for Research on Intercultural Cooperation at Tilburg University, Holland, and in 1985 he became professor of anthropology and international management at Maastrict University, also in Holland, teaching there until 1993. During this time he built on his research by examining the impact of the major religions on individualism versus group orientation, finding (not surprisingly) that Protestants score more strongly on the former and Catholics more on the latter. He also studied and wrote a paper on Confucian dynamism, to explain the rapid development of many Asian "tiger" economies, looking at the effects of Confucian teachings and ethics on thrift, perseverance, a sense of "face," and a belief in hierarchy.

Other academic researchers have explored Hofstede's theories from a more practical or region-specific focus. Another Dutch expert, **Fons Trompenaars**, concentrated on how national differences can be reconciled and integrated in a management context. **Gordon Redding**, formerly director of the business school at the University of Hong Kong and now a senior academic at the Euro-Asia Center at INSEAD, looked at how social and political forces in different parts of Asia influenced management cultures. His dimensions – post-colonialism, post-communism, and post-Confucianism – are explored in more detail in Chapter 3.

Transnational management structures and processes

If Hofstede and Trompenaars unpicked the cultural underpinnings of globalism, India-born **Sumantra Ghoshal**, strategy professor at INSEAD and London Business School, identified the accompanying structures and processes that provide the basis for most global training and development initiatives.

In partnership with a counterpart at Harvard Business School, **Christopher Bartlett**, Ghoshal analyzed in depth three types of borderless enterprise – the multinational (or "multidomestic"), the global, and the international – before settling on an ideal fourth, the transnational.

The multinational is essentially a federation of multiple national companies loosely connected across borders and largely managed by expatriates sent from the center. The global model is managed from the hub, benefiting from economies of scale in manufacturing and distribution. The international resembles the multinational but increasingly transfers its centrally produced technology and marketing business to its local businesses.

The ideal end point, the transnational, takes as its starting point the imperative identified by Percy Barnevik of Asea Brown Boveri that organizations need to "think global, act local." It combines local knowledge and a quick market response with global efficiency. In transnational corporations, knowledge transfer becomes more sophisticated; manufacturing, and research and development, are located in the most cost-efficient places; and there is serious training and knowledge to exploit unfamiliar markets.

To get a feel for the training and development implications of Ghoshal and Bartlett's theories, you have to understand two things. First, the transnational state is the ideal. Multinationals, and global and international corporations, throughout the 1990s and in the early years of the twenty-first century have striven to reach this state. Second, the mindset of key management and professional workers is nearly always one step behind the strategy, and the focus of most training and development initiatives has been to bring these workers up to speed.

So – drawing on the examples cited in this guide – the distance-learning MBA launched by Standard Chartered Bank in 1991 (see Chapter 4) was designed to help turn the organization from being one run largely by expatriates to one managed by a truly transnational team. Meanwhile, the "Spearhead China" initiative described in Chapter 6 was one of a series intended to transform Grand Metropolitan from a loose federation of largely unconnected businesses that withheld information from each other, even though they traded in the same countries, into an integrated food and drink conglomerate where ideas and new concepts were shared and developed centrally and locally – a process furthered significantly when GrandMet was incorporated into the recently merged Diageo Group.

GLOBALISM AND HR STRATEGY

The person who has most taken the thinking of Sumantra Ghoshal and Christopher Bartlett a stage further is **Dave Ulrich**, professor of business administration at the University of Michigan.

Ulrich has identified six capabilities that enable firms to "integrate and concentrate" global activities and also "separate and adapt" local activities. These are:

1 being able to determine core activities from non-core activities;
2 achieving consistency while allowing flexibility;
3 building global brand equity while honoring local customs;
4 obtaining leverage (bigger is better) while achieving focus (smaller is better);
5 sharing learning and creating new knowledge; and
6 engendering global perspective while ensuring local accountability.

Ulrich sees the HR function playing a critical role in enabling the organization to acquire these capabilities, for two reasons. First, the fifth capability (sharing learning and creating new knowledge) is a prerequisite to all the others and most likely to be achieved by training and development initiatives (see case study in *In Practice*).

As he puts it: "Staying competitive as you globalize requires developing the capabilities to share knowledge throughout the organization's far flung operations. Successful firms know the key to doing this is overcoming the 'not invented here' syndrome and providing the means to share learning across the world, whilst at the same time fostering the ability and motivation to generate new knowledge."

Second, the HR function can take each of the capabilities in turn and provide diagnostic tools for tracking how well the organization is proving in implementing them and what skills and qualities are required by front-line managers or supervisors. "It is imperative that HR practices are not only aligned with the capabilities needed to manage global operations, but integrated with each other." For example, he argues, if hiring local employees becomes important for adapting to local customs (see Chapter 3) then the training, compensation, and communication practices must also encourage this capability.

Ulrich's theories are reflected in a more front-line way by **Jack Welch**, former chairman and chief executive of General Electric and, according to *Fortune* magazine, "the greatest manager of the 20th century." Among the many ideas championed by Welch at GE, which have since become business management gospel, is the imperative that large corporations become "boundaryless" by capturing and "cross-fertilizing" best practice on a global scale.

Welch used the GE corporate training center at Crotonville (see Chapter 7), which all managers attended, and "action workouts" – where brainstorming and exchange of ideas between workers and managers happened in the workplace rather than off-site – to build a learning organization in which people in different industries and countries could learn from each other. This was reinforced by training and development concepts such as "reverse mentoring," with a young computer-literate staff bringing senior managers up to speed on technology.

However, the exchange that took place in the emerging economies of Central and Eastern Europe and Asia that GE expanded into in the early 1990s was far more one-sided than Welch, or anyone else at GE, liked to admit. Staff at the GE-acquired light bulb manufacturer Tungsram in Hungary, for instance, saw very little difference between Welch-inspired nostrums like "six sigma" and "workout" and the kind of exhortations to greater productivity they had endured under communist managers (see Chapter 3). In this sense, applying the models of Ghoshal and Bartlett, GE's activities were more redolent of an "international" company transferring its centrally produced technology and marketing expertise to local businesses than of a "transnational" enterprise drawing on the local knowledge of its workforce.

Management development across borders and boundaries

Jack Welch's concept of "boundarylessness" may not always have lived up to its high ideals in GE's romp across the markets of newly enfranchised post-Cold War economies. But it has inspired good practice in other companies, especially in the car and airline industries where transfer of technology and knowledge between members is a key incentive to commit to the new relationship.

At a meeting of the European Forum for Management Development in October 1997, the president and CEO of Siemens Nixdorf **Gerhard Schulmeyer** spelt out the reasons why. He pointed out that in a global marketplace where "think global, act local" was the overriding imperative, the economic value of knowledge is not based on ownership but on its use; and that the social ties that are so essential to the transfer and use of knowledge develop outside conventional work structures.

In these circumstances, training and development strategies based on "organizational charts and traditional workflows" will not help the organization to capture, transfer and use essential knowledge and good practice. It has to create links between new and more intangible "communities" of thought that not only encompass "global and local [corporate communities]" but "virtual and real [modes of relationship]" and "powerful and lost [groups of workers]."

What this actually means in practice has been illustrated by the training and development strategy designed by Lufthansa to transfer essential knowledge and good practice to other members of the Star Alliance – a consortium of national airlines that includes Air Canada and United Airlines in North America, Lufthansa and Scandinavian Airlines (SAS) in Europe, and Thai Airlines and South America's Varig in other parts of the world.

The strategy, explored in more detail in the section Chapter 7, includes international roadshows to communicate the ideas and vision of the alliance, and cross-cultural workshops and management development programs designed to help participants combine a cognitive understanding of the management issues with the management skills necessary to confront them.

The architect, human resources director **Thomas Sattelberger**, stresses that the overriding goal is to create a common identity between employees from different companies in the Star Alliance – staff that span different nationalities, cultures, and traditions.

He stresses that cultural identity is not a zero-sum struggle. "I can look at myself in many ways," he says. "I feel Bavarian because I am a citizen of Bavaria. I feel German because I have German nationality. I feel

European because my country is part of the European Union. Equally, managers and employees in the new initiative are asking themselves whether they are part of Lufthansa Cargo, the Lufthansa Group or the Star Alliance. The key question for us is how we can create a common sense of identity and purpose among flight attendants in Chicago, purchasing agents in India and maintenance staff in Beijing – and thus ensure common standards of reliability and quality across the whole network."

THE BROADER SOCIAL ROLE OF GLOBAL BUSINESS

The protests outside the perimeters of successive World Trade Organization conferences and Davos seminars have raised issues that will, in the short term, impact little on the global training and development activities of leading transnational organizations. However, corporate social policy has been a popular feature of the core or elective curriculum of top international MBA programs and a regular feature on boardroom education initiatives – and so it is worth highlighting some of the more important current thinking on the subject.

The most original thinker on the subject is not an academic or a consultant or a practicing front-line manager. He is a diplomat. Formerly head of the policy planning staff at the Foreign and Commonwealth Office, **Robert Cooper** became the UK minister at Bonn and a leading independent thinker on foreign affairs, contributing to successive Davos seminars and other meetings of minds between business leaders and international politicians.

Cooper argues that in the "post-modern" world, where computer software is increasingly more important than military hardware, the battles of tomorrow between states will be about whose industrial standards will achieve global acceptance. The weapons in these battles will be money and marketing muscle. As software replaces hardware – in the advanced part of the world – so markets replace military activity.

"Today's technology is primarily neither about land, nor about raw materials," he stresses. "In years gone by the world's richest man owned land. Then he owned oil. Now he owns ideas. Ideas and organisation make people rich, not materials. Note how many of the most successful entrepreneurs are software developers."

In this new vision of the world, how a company conducts itself in its relationships with foreign governments and investors is also critical. **Carlos Fortin** of the United Nations Conference on Trade and Development set out a few guidelines, based on UN policies, in 1994. They included:

» refraining, or continuing to refrain, from interference in purely domestic affairs;
» making deliberate efforts to ensure that company strategies and operations are fully consistent with national objectives and policies;
» showing flexibility in dealing with requests for local participation in ownership and control;
» bringing in capital from abroad, rather than pre-empting local financial resources;
» effectively transferring technologies adapted to local conditions and opportunities, and contributing to human resource development in sound infrastructure;
» maximizing the utilization of local labor and other inputs, and permitting local participation in the capital and management of local affiliates;
» promoting export capacity and, as appropriate, efficient substitution for imports;
» abstaining from tax evasion and abusive pricing transfer; and
» behaving in general as good corporate citizens.

These principles of "good" global business in the moral as well as the commercial sense of the world are mirrored in the Japanese philosophy *kyosei* championed through the 1990s by the chairman of Canon, **Ryuzaburo Kaku**.

Kaku argues, a bit like Sumantra Ghoshal, that companies go through four stages of moral and commercial advancement: benefiting and enriching the owners (including shareholders); focusing on the needs of employees; acting in stakeholders' interests; and addressing international interests. It is only when they reach the fifth stage – considering how they can contribute to a better world – that they can be said to be practicing *kyosei*.

In practice, argues Kaku, this means locating plants in countries with large trade imbalances; encouraging procurement from local plants as a way of reducing Japanese imports into these countries; setting up partnerships with competitor companies; and refusing to conduct research and development in fields that support aggressive military purposes or that will harm the environment.

KEY LEARNING POINTS

» Social, religious, and political forces shape an individual's response to any business theory requiring changes to behavior, management style, or hierarchy. How people respond to uncertainty, the distribution of power and status, and collective or individual styles of working are key differentials. (Hofstede/Trompenaars/Redding)

» Globalism is not uniform. Companies enter international markets in varying states of domestically determined integration, and these will determine their ability to maintain a coherent transnational overview of their business while responding effectively to local market needs. (Ghoshal/Bartlett)

» Global HR management, particularly training and development, will help an organization measure its progress in achieving truly transnational goals and the necessary exchange of ideas and concepts between the center and local operations that underpins them. (Ulrich/Welch/Schulmeyer/Sattelberger)

» The dominant role international companies play as engines of social transformation in the developing world brings with it new responsibilities that extend well beyond commercial growth and a narrow accountability to investors and stock markets. (Cooper/Fortin/Kaku)

FURTHER READING

Ghoshal, S. & Bartlett, C.A. (1989) *Managing across Borders: The transnational solution*. Harvard Business School Press, Boston.

Ghoshal, S. & Bartlett, C.A. (1998) *The Individualized Corporation: A fundamentally new approach to management*. Heinemann, London.

Hofstede, G. (2001) *Culture's Consequences: Comparing values, behaviors, institutions, and organizations across nations*, 2nd edn. Sage Publications, London and Thousand Oaks, California.

Redding, G. & Armitage, C. (1993) *Management Development in Asia-Pacific*. Economist Intelligence Unit, Hong Kong.

Welch, J.F. (2001) *Jack: Straight from the gut*. Warner Books, New York.

Cooper, R. (1998) "No longer out of the barrel of a gun." *MBA: The magazine for business masters*, January.

Hofstede, G. (1988) "Confucius and economic growth: new trends in culture's consequences." *Organizational Dynamics*, **16**: 4.

Kennedy, C. (1998) "Kyosei and the fifth corporation." *MBA: The magazine for business masters*, January.

Syrett, M. (1997) "Lufthansa: crossing virtual boundaries." *Forum*, **97**: 3.

Syrett, M. (1997) "Siemens Nixdorf: changing rules in economies and organisations." *Forum*, **97**: 3.

Taylor, W. (1991) "The logic of global business: an interview with ABB's Percy Barnevik." *Harvard Business Review*, March–April.

Ulrich, D. & Stewart Black, J. (1999) "The new frontier of global HR," in P. Joynt & B. Morton (eds) *The Global HR Manager*. Institute of Personnel and Development, London.

Fortin, C. (1994) The drivers of world prosperity. Stockton lecture, London Business School.

Resources

» Courses, programs, and partnerships
» Books
» E-learning providers

This chapter provides an extensive guide to using external suppliers like business schools and consultancies, a topic that has not been covered in any depth elsewhere in the guide. It also lists relevant contact details, as well as books and Websites. Some related publications are listed in the ExpressExec title *Management Development*.

COURSES, PROGRAMS, AND PARTNERSHIPS

Partnerships with external training and development suppliers have transformed global training and development more than any other field of management. The offerings neatly divide into those that help develop key professional technical and managerial staff, which have been largely undertaken by the prestigious international business schools, and those that develop front-line workers on a local level, which has been the realm of specialist consultancies.

Business schools and management centers

The evolution of globalism in business schools echoes Shakespeare. Some were born international, some sought international status, and some had internationalism thrust upon them. In the first category – those born global – are the two organically international schools based in Europe, Lausanne's IMD and Fontainebleau's INSEAD.

INSEAD was founded in 1957 in the wake of the treaty that established the European Economic Community. IMD (the International Institute for Management Development) was set up in 1991 from a merger of two corporate schools, IMI (the International Management School) and IMEDE (l'Institut pour les Méthodes de Direction d'Enterprises), sponsored by Alcan and Nestlé respectively.

Both were established outside the educational systems of their host countries. Although INSEAD tended to draw heavily on US staff and methods in its early years and IMD is more pan-European than truly international, the two schools were freer to establish a genuinely international perspective in the three key areas of faculty, students, and teaching materials than most of their domestically oriented counterparts in other parts of the developed world. Issues that were little covered by the Anglo-Saxon business education model – such as sustaining effective family enterprises and cross-cultural management – were examined in depth. Indeed one of the reasons why the two schools joined forces with the European Foundation for Management Development to found a new business school in Shanghai in 1991, the China Europe International Business School, was to counter the US/UK model in a region where enduring family dynasties and cross-cultural tensions are key business issues.

The second category of schools – those that have actively sought international status – emerged in the late 1980s. A coterie of previously domestically oriented schools – most notably London Business School, Wharton School (University of Pennsylvania), Columbia Business School, and the Fuqua School of Business (Duke University) – realizing that the companies who sponsored them were expanding rapidly into international markets, overhauled their recruitment policies and the core curriculum of their flagship MBA and executive programs to reflect this. In their wake came a number of national schools in Europe, most notably Groupe ESC Lyon in France, the Erasmus Graduate School of Business in Holland, and IESE and ESADE in Spain.

Currently, in terms of their success, it is a mixed bag. Most have internationalized their faculties and teaching materials but (arguably) only London Business School has an international student body that ranks alongside those of INSEAD and IMD. The biggest progress in degree programs has been in executive MBA programs targeted at company-sponsored senior managers at the top of their organizations rather than self-sponsored students in mid-career. Fuqua's Global Executive MBA has been a noteworthy trailblazer, notable for sustaining and extending the learning between modules through the use of Internet group work (see Chapter 5).

The third category of schools – those that have had internationalism thrust upon them – originally based their competitive strategy on developing an expertise in distance learning and very quickly found that this dragged them, willing or not, into the international arena. The Open University Business School (OUBS), originally a very domestic affair, found in the 1980s that although its students were still UK-based, they appreciated a qualification they could take while moving from one geographical location to another. It was then only a small step to extend the service to other nationalities.

In 1994 OUBS went the whole way by launching a new initiative giving international students the opportunity to study on the same course wherever they were based in Europe, and to continue doing so even if they moved from one country to another. While they pushed out the boundaries from Western Europe to Central and Eastern Europe, schools like Henley Management College, Warwick Business School, and Strathclyde Business School (along with a patchwork of Australian schools like Curtin Business School, the Australian Graduate School of Management, and the Murdoch Business School) were doing the same in Singapore, Hong Kong, and East Asian "hub" cities like Shanghai.

From the point of view of this guide, it is the capacity of most of these schools to work with clients designing in-company and consortium programs, which enables professional, technical, and management staff from around the world to acquire global management expertise, that is most noteworthy. Henley, for example, has used its distance-learning and Internet-based learning technology to design and deliver in-company programs for international companies such as Standard Chartered Bank and Cable & Wireless – and these initiatives are covered in depth in Chapter 5.

The global business consortium program run by London Business School is another example. This brings together world-class companies like Asea Brown Boveri, Lufthansa, and SKF to help develop a generation of leaders capable of leading their organizations into the next phase of global development.

Like the Henley and Fuqua programs, the emphasis is on participants learning from each other, comparing with managers from other member companies the ways in which their own organization manages large complex businesses, expands their presence in emerging markets, and manages across borders. Each module of the program, attended by six managers nominated by each member company, starts with a session on the creation and delivery of global strategy, covering issues such as effective joint-venture management and global people management.

From this global picture, the program focuses on how consortium companies should manage their response to local issues and developments through face-to-face discussions with leading politicians, academics, and front-line managers from Asia, South America, and Europe. A final session in each module helps companies explore how they can assimilate the new ideas and issues into their own long-term strategy.

This "curriculum" is supported by a number of exercises designed to reinforce the team-based approach to learning. Company teams prepare an analysis of their own company and present it during the first module. Cross-company teams are each assigned a company to focus on, and have the opportunity for an in-depth discussion with the CEO during the final module.

Two days of each module are spent examining how specific consortium members have created a competitive advantage in one region of the world. In 1998, for example, the managers from Standard Chartered Bank described how they had built up their banking operations in Asia, and listened to presentations from SKF on their manufacturing strategy in São Paulo, from British Telecom on their strategy for entry into the global market, and from Lufthansa on their alliance with their Brazilian partner Varig.

As a way of helping participants translate what they have learned on the program back to their own jobs, the tutors issue a "CEO challenge." This forms the basis for work by participants from the same company throughout the program and culminates in a presentation to their own CEO in the final module.

Standard Chartered Bank's six members in 1998 were given the task of understanding the Japanese market; SKF's managers were given the task of building a second "brand" for the company; LG's managers were asked to present proposals for how their company could develop a more effective alliance structure; while those from Lufthansa were given the task of developing a strategy for the next stage of their ambitious Star Alliance.

With over 30 participants having taken part in the program each year since its inception in 1995, the program is developing a sizeable body of alumni, who are now being tapped as a further source of learning and support. An alumni day was being launched at the time of writing. Alumni are also asked to support new participants and take part in case presentations.

In the same way, the program has developed its own dedicated source of training materials. "We change the content each year to fit in with the developments in each company and the rather dramatic changes in the commercial environment in which they operate," says the program director Professor Lynda Gratton. "But what makes the learning so effective is our ability to relate this to the case presentations made by the participants themselves. We have now started to take this material and write it up as formal case studies for future use on the program."

Consultancies

In global training terms, consultancies tend to divide into two types: general consultancies, whose international training activities are a by-product of a larger strategy or technological project, and specialist consultancies, who usually confine their activities to a particular concept or method of training. Some in both categories have a global reach and can offer international companies cross-regional support. Others are local to one country or region.

To gain a feel for the international training work undertaken by consultancies, let's look at a cross section of projects recently undertaken in Asia.

» A business training project was undertaken by the Poon Kam Kai Institute of Management – an outreach consultancy affiliated to the University of Hong Kong – for the Hong Kong Aircraft Engineering Company. This assignment involved taking 400 of the company's engineers and specialist technicians, and putting them through an intensive program of tailored business education directly linked to the company's drive to create new markets for its services in mainland China – in direct competition with North American, European, and Asian rivals.

» A "train the trainers" exercise was conducted by the UK-based Ashridge Consulting Group for Malaysia Airlines (MAS), designed to support the airline's own total quality management (TQM) initiative. Working with Ashridge tutors, 15 senior MAS managers were trained in the basic concepts and techniques arising from the initiative. These managers in turn cascaded the processes downwards to functional directors, middle managers, flight and cabin crew, and union representatives. Ashridge was involved at each stage, helping to train and develop multidisciplinary teams to deal with key areas of improvement.

» A quality management exercise was conducted by Forum Asia for China's Kowloon and Canton Railway Corporation (KCRC). It required Forum staff to work with senior KCRC managers to gain consensus among front-line staff for a set of values that subsequently underpinned a highly successful TQM program.

A further exercise for KCRC, undertaken by PA Consulting, helped the company upgrade its mobile radio system. The project involved PA consultants training KCRC staff in how to assess and identify user requirements, design future specifications, manage the tender process, and negotiate effectively with suppliers.

As you can see from the cross section of institutions in the list above, the market for global training has overlapped suppliers. A typical tender, depending on its nature, might include an international business school, an independent management center, an international business consultancy, or a specialist training firm. The cross-fertilization between academic institutions, consultancies, and sole practitioners is positively incestuous. Some schools, like the UK's Ashridge Management College, have their own outreach consultancy firm benefiting from the same brand. Many consultancies, like the US-based Harbridge House, were founded by business school academics. Business gurus attached to one or more schools now run their own consultancies in parallel, often competing with the very institutions they work for. Gary Hamel's California-based firm Strategos is a case in point.

This often leaves the internal HR consultants managing the tender comparing apples with pears. Below is a checklist of what to look for in a global training supplier.

» Does the supplier have a history of work (and a track record of success) in the country or region where the initiative is to take place and/or in the relevant industry or sector?
» Does the project team provided by the supplier include tutors or trainers who have lived or worked in the region and/or have ethnic ties that will give them insights into the cross-cultural complexities? Will these team members be acceptable to trainees from the sites involved? (Training consultancy projects have broken down because of inter-regional prejudices – such as when Czech trainers are used with Slovak employees, or Hong Kong tutors with mainlanders.)

» Has the supplier conducted academic or market research into the cross-cultural issues influencing the country where the initiative is to take place, and demonstrated effectively how they will respond to them?

More generally, whether you are seeking a domestic or an international supplier, it is worth checking the following.

» Does the supplier have skill in client liaison, and the ability to identify or question your true development needs?
» Will you get access to the real McCoy – senior faculty or consultants with expert research and teaching ability – and not just an understudy?
» Does the supplier just "press button B" – outlining general statements of truth and established points of principle – or is the supplier prepared to get to know the individual or organization well enough to use their intellectual resources to uncover hidden insights?
» Is the "big noise" – the star member of faculty or practice – prepared to work with you to tailor or design the optimum program, or will you wind up with a verbal synopsis of his or her latest book or research program?
» Whose diary is it anyway? – are you calling the tune on timings and venue, or are they merely fitting you in?

Contact details

American Assembly of Collegiate Schools of Business (AACSB), 600 Emerson Road, Suite 300, St Louis MO 63141-6762, United States. Tel: +1 314 872 8481; Fax: +1 314 872 8495; Website: www.aacsb.edu
Anderson School at UCLA, 110 Westwood Plaza, Box 951481, Los Angeles CA 90095-1481, United States. Tel: +1 310 825 6944; Fax: +1 310 825 8582; Website: www.anderson.ucla.edu
Arthur D. Little School of Management, 194 Beacon Street, Chestnut Hill MA 012167, United States. Tel: +1 617 552 2877; Fax: +1 617 552 2051; E-mail: adlschool.mgmt@adlittle.com; Website: www.adlsom.com
Ashridge Management College, Ashridge, Berkhamsted, Hertfordshire HP4 1NS, United Kingdom. Tel: +44 1442 841000; Fax: +44 1442 841306; E-mail: info@ashridge.org.uk

Association for Management Education and Development, 14–15 Belgrave Square, London SW1X 8PS, United Kingdom. Tel: +44 207 235 3505; Fax: +44 207 235 3565; E-mail: amed.office@net.demon.co.uk

Association of Business Schools, 344–54 Gray's Inn Road, London WC1X 8BP, United Kingdom. Tel: +44 207 837 1899; Fax: +44 207 837 8189; E-mail: 106262.227@compuserve.com; Website: www.leeds.ac. uk/bes/abs/abshome.htm

Association of Management Development Institutions in South Asia, 8-2-333/A Road no. 3, Banjara Hill, Hyderabad 500034, India. Tel: +91 40 244089; Fax: +91 40 244801

Association of MBAs, 15 Duncan Terrace, London N1 8BZ, United Kingdom. Tel: +44 207 837 3375; Fax: +44 207 278 3634

Business Association of Latin American Studies, c/o School of Business Administration, University of San Diego, 5998 Alcala Park, San Diego CA 92110, United States. Tel: +1 619 604836; Fax: +1 619 2604891; E-mail: dimon@acusd.edu

Central and East European Management Development Association, Brdo pri Kranju, 4000 Kranj, Slovenia. Tel: +386 64 221 761; Fax: +386 64 222 070; E-mail: ceeman@iedc-brdo.si

Centre for High Performance Development, Elvetham Hall, Hartley Wintney, Hampshire RG27 8AS, United Kingdom. Tel: +44 1252 842677; Fax: +44 1252 842564; E-mail: info@chpd.co.uk

Chartered Institute of Personnel and Development, CIPD House, Camp Road, London SW19 4UX, United Kingdom. Tel: +44 208 971 9000

China Europe International Business School, Jiaotong University, Minhang Campus, 800 Dong Chuan Road, Shanghai 200240, People's Republic of China. Tel: +8621 6463 0200; Fax: +8621 6435 8928

Chinese University of Hong Kong, Faculty of Business Administration, Leung Kau Kui Building, Shatin, New Territories, Hong Kong, People's Republic of China. Tel: +852 609 7642; Fax: +852 603 5762

City University Business School, Frobisher Crescent, Barbican Centre, London EC2Y 8HB, United Kingdom. E-mail: cubs-postgrad@city.ac.uk; Website: www.city.ac.uk/cubs

Columbia Business School, Uris Hall, 3022 Broadway, New York NY 10027, United States. Tel: +1 212 854 1961; Fax: +1 212 662 6754; Website: www.columbia.edu

Cranfield School of Management, Cranfield, Bedford MK43 0AL, United Kingdom. Tel: +44 1234 751122; Fax: +44 1234 751806; Website: www.cranfield@ac.uk/som

EM Lyon, 23 avenue Guy de Collongue, BP 174, 69132 Ecully Cedex, France. Tel: +33 4 7833 7865; Fax: +33 4 7833 6169; Website: www.em-lyon.com

European Foundation for Management Development, 88 rue Gachard, B-1050 Brussels, Belgium. Tel: +32 2 648 0385; Fax: +32 2 646 0768; E-mail: info@efmd.be; Website: www.efmd.be

European Institute for Advanced Studies in Management, Rue d'Egmont 13, B-1000 Brussels, Belgium. Tel: +32 2 511 9116; Fax: +32 2 512 1929

Graduate Management Admission Council, 8300 Greensboro Drive Suite 750, McLean VA 22102, United States. Tel: +1 703 749 0131; Fax: +1 703 749 169; E-mail: gmacmail@gmac.com; Website: www.gmac.org

Haas School of Business, University of California at Berkeley, S440 Student Services Building, No. 1902, Berkeley CA 94720-1902, United States. Tel: +1 510 642 1405; Fax: +1 510 643 6659; Website: www.haas. berkeley.edu

Harvard Business School, Soldiers Field Road, Boston MA 02163, United States. Tel: +1 617 495 6127; Fax: +1 617 496 9272; Website: www.hbs.edu

HEC School of Management, 1 rue de la Libération, 78351 Jouy-en-Josas Cedex, France. Tel: +33 1 3967 7379/7382; Fax: +33 1 3967 7465, Website: www.hec.fr

Henley Management College, Greenlands, Henley-on-Thames, Oxfordshire RG9 3AU, United Kingdom. Tel: +44 1491 571454; Fax: +44 1491 571635; E-mail: info@henley.co.uk; Website: www.henleymc. ac.uk

IESE (International Graduate School of Management), University of Navarra, Avenida Pearson 21, 08034 Barcelona, Spain. Tel: +34 93 253 4229; Fax: +34 93 253 4343; Website: www.iese.edu

IMD (International Institute for Management Development), Chemin de Bellerive 23, PO Box 915, CH 1001 Lausanne, Switzerland. Tel: +44 41 21 618 0111; Fax: +44 41 21 618 0707; E-mail: info@imd.ch; Website: www.imd.ch

Imperial College Management School, 53 Prince's Gate, Exhibition Road, London SW7 2PG, United Kingdom. Tel: +44 207 594 9205; Fax: +44 207 823 7685; E-mail: m.school@ic.ac.uk; Website: http://ms. ic.ac.uk

INSEAD, Boulevard de Constance, 77305 Fontainebleau Cedex, France. Tel: +33 1 6072 4000; Fax: +33 1 6074 5500; Website: www.insead.fr/

Institute for Employment Studies, Mantell Building, University of Sussex, Brighton BN1 9RF, United Kingdom. Tel: +44 1273 686751; Fax: +44 1273 690430

Judge Institute of Management, University of Cambridge, Trumpington Street, Cambridge CB2 1AG, United Kingdom. Tel: +44 1223 337051/2/3; Fax: +44 1223 339581; Website: www.jims.cam.ac. uk/mba

Leonard N. Stern School of Business, New York University, 44 West 4th Street, New York NY 10012-1126, United States. Tel: +1 212 998 0600; Fax: +1 212 995 4231; Website: www.stern.nyu.edu

London Business School, Sussex Place, Regent's Park, London NW1 4SA, United Kingdom. Tel: +44 207 262 5050; Fax: +44 207 724 7875; Website: www.lbs.ac.uk

Manchester Business School, Booth Street West, Manchester M15 6PB, United Kingdom. Tel: +44 161 275 7139; Fax: +44 161 275 6556; Website: www.mbs.ac.uk

MIT Sloan School of Management, Massachusetts Institute of Technology, 50 Memorial Drive, Cambridge MA 02142, United States. Tel: +1 617 253 3730; Fax: +1 617 253 6405; Website: http://mitsloan. mit.edu

Open University Business School, Walton Hall, Milton Keynes MK7 6AA, United Kingdom. Tel: +44 1908 653449; Fax: +44 1908 654320; Website: www.oubs.open.ac.uk

Roffey Park Management Institute, Forest Road, Horsham, West Sussex, United Kingdom. Tel: +44 1293 851644; Fax: +44 1293 851565; E-mail: info@roffey-park.co.uk

SDA Bocconi, Masters Division, Via Balilla 16–18, 20136 Milan, Italy. Tel: +39 2 5836 3281; Fax: +39 2 5836 3275; Website: www.sda.uni-bocconi.it

Stanford Graduate School of Business, 518 Memorial Way, Stanford University, Stanford CA 94305-5015, United States. Tel: +1 650 723 2766; Fax: +1 650 725 7831; Website: http://gsb-www.stanford.edu

Strathclyde Graduate School of Business, 199 Cathedral Street, Glasgow G4 0QU, United Kingdom. Tel: +44 141 553 6118/9; Fax: +44 141 552 8851; Website: www.strath.ac.uk/gsb/index.html

Sundridge Park Management Centre, Plaistow Lane, Bromley, Kent BR1 3TP, United Kingdom. Tel: +44 208 313 3131

University of Michigan Business School, 701 Tappan Street, Ann Arbor MI 48109-1234, United States. Tel: +1 734 763 5796; Fax: +1 734 763 7804; Website: www.bus.umich.edu

Warwick Business School, University of Warwick, Coventry CV4 7AL, United Kingdom. Tel: +44 1203 523922; Fax: +44 1203 524643; Website: www.wbs.warwick.ac.uk

Wharton School, University of Pennsylvania, 102 Vance Hall, 3733 Spruce Street, Philadelphia PA 19104-6374, United States. Tel: +1 215 898 6183; Fax: +1 215 898 0120; Website: www.wharton.upenn.edu

BOOKS

On cross-cultural management

Hofstede, G. (2001) *Culture's Consequences: Comparing values, behaviors, institutions, and organizations across nations*, 2nd edn. Sage Publications, London and Thousand Oaks, California.

Hofstede, G.J., Pedersen, P.B., & Hofstede, G. (2002) *Exploring Culture: Exercises, stories and synthetic cultures*. Nicholas Brealey, London.

Two bibles written by the god of cross-cultural management, Geert Hofstede. The first, *Culture's Consequences*, brings together the findings of a lifetime's survey of front-line staff using a diagnostic survey first developed when he was chief psychologist at IBM. The original edition, published in 1980, was based on the responses to 100,000 questionnaires by IBM managers in 72 countries. The 2001 edition updates the conclusions by incorporating responses to the same questionnaire by managers Hofstede has worked with in more recent academic posts at international business schools such as IMD in Lausanne, INSEAD in Fontainebleau, and the Institute for Research on Intercultural Cooperation at Tilburg University, which he helped to found.

Exploring Culture explores the management implications of cross-cultural cooperation, including insights on program design and delivery based on Hofstede's work at INSEAD and IMD. Hofstede's theories are explored in detail in Chapter 8 of this ExpressExec guide.

On global organizational structure and corporate culture

Ghoshal, S. & Bartlett, C.A. 1989 *Managing across Borders: The transnational solution*. Harvard Business School Press, Boston.

Ghoshal, S. & Bartlett, C.A. 1998 *The Individualized Corporation: A fundamentally new approach to management*. Heinemann, London.

Managing across Borders, still a classic, was the first attempt to analyze the different ways in which companies were expanding into international markets, and the impact this was having on their structure and culture. Published before the great surge into developing economies in the early 1990s, unleashed by the collapse of communist-inspired command economies, it anticipated many of the fundamental changes this brought to how business generally is conducted. The way the authors categorize international companies, and the implications this has for global training and development strategies, is examined at length in Chapter 6 of this ExpressExec title.

Ghoshal and Bartlett's more recent book *The Individualized Corporation* championed the concept of a "new moral contract" to replace the older "psychological contract" envisaged by the US guru Frederick Herzberg. In this new version, each employee takes responsibility for his or her "best in class" performance and continuous learning, while the corporation undertakes the opportunity for that learning. Although this is territory more relevant to other ExpressExec titles, in particular *Developing the Individual* and *The Innovative Individual*, its impact on global training and development is also profound. The author's main contention – that there is a rising tide of autonomy among workers that will pose a huge problem for big companies – is spectacularly pertinent to global corporations. This is because the level of autonomy, as measured by Geert Hofstede's cultural indicators (see Chapter 8 of this ExpressExec guide), will vary from one region to another, making consistent employee communication and training and development policies across the company almost impossible to achieve.

On globalization and human resource management

Joynt, P. & Morton, B. (eds) (1999) *The Global HR Manager*. Institute of Personnel and Development, London.

Although this book covers a whole gamut of issues connected with globalism, its coverage of training and development-related concepts and good practice is particularly good. It argues that, while basic training and development methods are the same the world over, a wholly different mindset is required by HR managers responsible for coordinating these activities. The challenges range from the training implications of moving key employees from one region to another at short notice, through helping them operate in a completely alien environment and developing international teams, to the evolution of radically new ways of working.

Well worth reading in its own right is the chapter contributed by the University of Michigan's Dave Ulrich and his colleague J. Stewart Black from the Asia Pacific HR Partnership. Entitled "The new frontier of global HR," it stresses the importance of sharing learning and creating new knowledge across geographical and cultural boundaries if organizations are really to "think global, act local" (see Chapter 8 of this ExpressExec title).

E-LEARNING PROVIDERS

E-learning has played a central role in expanding the reach of global training initiatives. Among business schools, Internet-based technology has transformed what is and is not impossible (see above and Chapter 5). Other providers, however, remain surprisingly domestic in what they currently offer. But the inventory below (Table 9.1), compiled by Albert Vicere at Pennsylvania State University, lists providers with the technological capacity to work in partnership with companies in designing tailor-made initiatives, which will help achieve many of the goals outlined in this guide.

Table 9.1 E-learning providers who specialize in designing tailor-made initiatives.

Organization name and address	Description from Website
AthenaOnline www.athenaonline.com	"AthenaOnline is a premier publisher of multimedia training, education and career development products. We are an Internet 'knowledge network' headquartered in the San Francisco Bay Area, California."
Centra www.centra.com	"Web-based software and services for live collaboration, enabling business interaction, collaborative commerce and corporate learning."
Click2learn www.click2learn.com	"A leading provider of full service e-Learning solutions to businesses, government agencies, and educational institutions throughout the world."
Corporate University Xchange www.corpu.com	"A corporate education research and consulting firm that assists organisations in optimising their learning resources."
DigitalThink www.digitalthink.com	"DigitalThink is the leader in designing, developing, and deploying e-learning solutions to Fortune 1000 companies."
Docent www.docent.com	"Docent is a provider of e-Learning products and services that enable the Web-based exchange of personalised and measurable knowledge within and among large enterprises, education content providers and professional communities."
Eduventures.com www.eduventures.com	"Eduventures.com Inc is a provider of education technology industry analysis, market data and insight to buyers, suppliers and users of e- learning products and services."
Executive Development Associates www.edanetworks.com	"Executive Development Associates (EDA) is a leading education and consulting firm specialising in the strategic use of executive/leadership development."

(*continued overleaf*)

Table 9.1 (*continued*)

Organization name and address	Description from Website
Forum Corporation www.forum.com	"A global leader in workplace learning . . . pioneering new ways to achieve business results through learning. We specialise in creating innovative solutions that help companies build competitive advantage and lasting customer loyalty."
FT Knowledge www.ftknowledge.com	"FT Knowledge is one of the world's leading providers of business education and management development. We specialise in providing learning and development that is highly relevant to the needs of business and those who work within it."
Institute for Management Studies www.ims-online.com	"A leader in executive education and management development for over 25 years, IMS holds one-day workshops on cutting edge management issues, taught by leading business school professors from the graduate schools at Harvard, University of Pennsylvania, UC Berkeley, Penn State, Stanford, SMU, Georgetown and others."
Knowledge Universe www.knowledgeu.com	"Knowledge Universe (KU) operates, incubates and invests in leading companies that build human capital by helping organisations and individuals to realise their full potential."
Parthenon Group www.parthenon.com	"The Parthenon Group . . . provide[s] strategic advisory consulting services to business leaders who demand seasoned counsel and seek true business insights that yield results."
Pensare www.pensare.com	"Pensare develops Knowledge Community on line learning solutions that drive teamwork, creativity and business results through the innovative use of strategic

Table 9.1   (*continued*)

Organization name and address	Description from Website
	alliances, validated content, leading technology, applied learning tools, human interaction and cultural adaptation."
Provant www.provant.com	"We provide integrated solutions that resolve performance-based organisational challenges."
Quisic www.quisic.com	"Your freeline resource for the most current business thinking on the web. Business education solutions for corporations and academic institutions."
Saba www.saba.com	"Saba is a leading provider of e-learning infrastructure, which consists of Internet-based learning management systems, business to business learning exchanges and related services."
SmartForce www.smartforce.com	"SmartForce is redefining learning for the Internet age with its first of a kind, fully integrated, Internet-based e-Learning technology."
Tacit www.tacit.com	"Tacit Knowledge Systems, Inc, is a pioneer and leader in providing automated knowledge discovery and exchange systems that, for the first time, offer organisations automated access to explicit, tacit and even private knowledge."
The Learning Partnership www.tlp.org	"The Learning Partnership is owned by some of the world's leading business academies. Our mission is to create and share knowledge around the key issues facing business in the new Millennium."

Table 9.1 (*continued*)

Organization name and address	Description from Website
UNext www.unext.com	"UNext was created to deliver world class education. We are building a scalable education business that delivers the power of knowledge around the world."

Adapted from Vicere, A.A. (2000) "Ten observations on e-learning." *Human Resource Planning*, November.

Ten Steps to Making it Work

1 Link your training strategy to the company's global one
2 But do not underestimate the cross-cultural complexities
3 Choose the right champions
4 Choose the right suppliers
5 Make maximum use of new technology
6 But socialize the learning
7 Deliver training where it will most engage and inspire
8 Do not underestimate regional cross-cultural enmities
9 Keep your database up to date
10 See it as a journey

1. LINK YOUR TRAINING STRATEGY TO THE COMPANY'S GLOBAL ONE

Companies enter global markets in contrasting states of readiness. Most see global growth as a reflection of growth at home and conduct business abroad very much as they do at home.

The training strategy needs to reflect this. If the company has grown through acquisition and technology transfer to subsidiaries, then the training strategy that supported this domestic strategy will need to be adapted to encompass acquisition and technology transfer abroad. The same applies if the growth has been achieved organically, through commercial alliances or by individual joint ventures.

2. BUT DO NOT UNDERESTIMATE THE CROSS-CULTURAL COMPLEXITIES

Local workforces may be open to new methods and business concepts, but constrained by social and economic traditions that inhibit their ability to adapt. In societies where wealth and status (including management status) are determined by sex, education, age, political standing, and family background, staff may find it hard to accept Western business concepts of meritocracy and equal opportunities. In post-communist economies where central control and functional stratification were bedrocks of stability, staff may find cross-functional working and empowerment difficult to assimilate. They may also see notions of performance management and empowerment as little different from politically motivated exhortations for greater productivity of the communist days, to be ignored or sidelined.

The most overt cross-cultural problems were tackled in the mid-1990s. Many of the economic hotspots like mainland China, and the rapidly developing economies of Central and Eastern Europe like Hungary and Poland, have adapted to Western techniques and philosophies. But the problems have merely gone underground and are most likely to emerge during training and development exercises rather than in upfront negotiations. In HR terms, this means that training and organizational needs analysis exercises must be exceptionally rigorous in flushing out cross-cultural problems – likewise with post-training assessment and appraisal.

3. CHOOSE THE RIGHT CHAMPIONS

One of the most important lessons learned from early technology transfer exercises, undertaken by companies like General Electric and Volkswagen with newly acquired subsidiaries in developing countries, was that the skills and attitudes of the line managers spearheading the exercise were critical.

Specialists were chosen instead of experienced general managers. They concerned themselves with solving production and technological problems, not with the process of learning that local staff were going to have to undergo. Senior managers of the parent company's dominant nationality were made responsible for strategy development, leaving local managers with only operative tasks. The whole process was too task-oriented. Little attempt was made to gain cooperation through team-building and regular briefings with local staff.

In an age when "think global, act local" is the dominant philosophy, this just will not do. The reasons for acquiring or collaborating with subsidiary partners may be due to market presence, local infrastructure, or synergy at the top but – as with mergers and acquisitions at home – the ability to exploit the long-term advantages will be down to plain old-fashioned people management. Once the initial post-acquisition or post-agreement training is over, this is down to line managers exercising their skills in knowledge exchange on a day-to-day basis rather than carefully crafted centrally driven HR interventions.

4. CHOOSE THE RIGHT SUPPLIERS

Choosing the right training supplier is always a difficult consumer task, in an age when university business schools, independent management centers, general management consultancies, specialist training firms, and sole practitioners wind up on the same tender list. In global training projects, the criteria are even more complex.

Over and above the usual issues of whether the firm has the right methodology, expert knowledge, and client liaison skills, HR specialists will need to ask other questions. Does it have a history of work (and a track record of success) in the country or region where the initiative is to take place and/or in the relevant industry or sector? Does the project team provided by the supplier include tutors or trainers who have lived or worked in the region and/or have ethnic ties that will give them insights into the cross-cultural complexities? Will these team members be acceptable to trainees from the sites involved? (Training consultancy projects have broken down because of inter-regional prejudices – such as when Czech trainers are used with Slovak employees, or Hong Kong tutors with mainlanders.)

5. MAKE MAXIMUM USE OF NEW TECHNOLOGY

Global training and development is the field where new Internet technology has made the most difference. The ability to link up not just individuals but whole teams from different countries or regions to take part in sophisticated group work that would previously only have been possible face to face has transformed not only business school courses but in-company programs.

Personal computers and Internet access have penetrated developing countries more thoroughly than any other technology, particularly in "frontier" outposts of global capitalism like Russia, Central Asia, and mainland China. A new generation of workers is growing up that is used to establishing and sustaining personal relationships through the computer and at a distance, using text-messaging and other emerging media. The design and effective use of advanced intranets and discussion databases, like those used in Shell's knowledge exchange networks (see Chapter 5), makes it possible for formal learning to be sustained and captured between peers without HR or other central management interventions. This can build up over the years into an incalculably rich archive of material and intellectual property, which can in turn be used to develop firm-specific theories and case examples on future programs.

6. BUT SOCIALIZE THE LEARNING

Companies like Lufthansa and BBV (see Chapter 7) have found that inter-company roadshows and joint venues where employees from different partners or subsidiaries can "meet, greet, and eat" are as important as formal courses in developing a common understanding of the aims and objectives of commercial alliances, joint ventures, and new international initiatives.

There is a greater understanding of the role of serendipity in knowledge exchange and ideas creation, and this is particularly important in global business given the cross-cultural complexities that constrain it. This topic is explored in more detail in the ExpressExec guides *The Innovative Individual* and *Creativity*.

7. DELIVER TRAINING WHERE IT WILL MOST ENGAGE AND INSPIRE

That said, there are still compelling reasons why trainees in newly developing countries should be given access to training in other parts of the world and be able to sustain the benefits through good old-fashioned career management.

Companies like the Asia-based accountancy and consultancy giant Deloitte Touche Tohmatsu found in the cut-throat job markets of Singapore, Hong Kong, and Shanghai that the prospect of systematic long-term professional training – using a combination of strategic career development and short-term international transfers – was critical in enabling them to attract, retain, and properly exploit local or regional project teams.

A persistent problem, however, is that trainees from developing countries are invariably attracted by the prospect of courses and assignments in North America and Europe, over and above those in less developed parts of their own regions. Deloitte's regional human resources and training director Martyn Fisher comments: "We have always had to argue hard to convince local consultants that the emerging business opportunities are now in Asia and that they would therefore do better staying in the region. This is particularly difficult if the assignment is in a less developed economy. There is a tendency for them to think 'what am I going to learn from a place that is further behind technically?'" To combat this problem, Deloitte had to develop a new regional transfer scheme that combined training in North American or European centers with assignments in Asia.

8. DO NOT UNDERESTIMATE REGIONAL CROSS-CULTURAL ENMITIES

The complex history and rapid development of countries in the emerging world have created cross-cultural enmities that lurk below the surface and may not be immediately apparent from the outset.

Many Western companies thought that Hong Kong in the 1980s and early 1990s was an ideal gateway to commercial expansion on the mainland, providing a pool of well-educated labor that could be recruited and trained to be the vanguard. They were quickly disillusioned when they found that the mainland Chinese disliked Cantonese-speaking Southerners almost more than the "white devils" they were used to.

This quickly led to cut-throat demand for professionally educated Mandarin speakers from the Northern provinces, which resulted in 100 percent annual turnover rates in the mid-1990s, only recently alleviated in recent years by extensive in-company training. Very similar experiences were encountered in Central and Eastern Europe (for example between the Slovaks and Czechs) and in the still volatile republics of Central Asia that are attracting the next wave of Western investment.

9. KEEP YOUR DATABASE UP TO DATE

Training is a fast-moving world at the best of times but it is particularly volatile in the international arena, where suppliers dip in and out of particular regions on an almost annual basis.

The US consultancy Harbridge House used to have a thriving European practice that pioneered academic – company partnerships in tailored degrees and executive courses. Italy's Ambrosetti Consulting Group broke new ground in international boardroom development in California and London. Both have now pulled out of overseas markets. The pioneering tailored-program specialists of the early 1990s in Hong Kong, the Poon Kam Kai Institute of Management, still exists but has experienced a total staff turnover.

The reputation and capability of consultancies in developing regions can rest on the skill and personal contacts of one to two key individuals, and the consequences of taking anything on trust can be disastrous. A module in South China organized by a local consultancy for London Business School's International Executive Masters Program broke down completely because, misunderstanding the business world's use of the word "school," the local organizers in China laid on trips suitable for college students with junior party officials or tourist guides as hosts rather than with senior executives capable of answering the sophisticated questions posed by the participants, who all held strategic positions in their own organizations. Given the complex network of contacts involved, there was no way that the head of the program could have checked out the situation on the ground in advance.

So, regularly revisit your list of suppliers and check out their progress personally. Your reputation will be on the line as well as theirs if you act in ignorance.

10. SEE IT AS A JOURNEY

As BMW's Klaus Bodel stresses in Chapter 7, globalization is a journey and the training initiatives that support it are no exception. A great deal has happened very quickly during the last decade. Top-down technology transfer in the field has been replaced by knowledge exchange and Internet learning. Most of the alliances, mergers, and joint ventures used to launch the process are less than ten years old. Countries like China and Russia are beginning to adapt and even adopt Western management methods.

But the creation of multinational teams and global task forces has in turn created new and unforeseen learning needs. The balance in the control and flow of expertise between the "center" and local operations fluctuated widely from one decade to the next in the latter half of the twentieth century. The creation of virtual structures that has been such a focus for the General Electric and Lufthansa corporate universities has not even begun to impact on this swaying balance. But whatever needs and demands are engendered, you can be sure that training and development, in whatever form, will be required to meet them.

Frequently Asked Questions (FAQs)

Q1: What is meant by "global" training and development?

A: First, you need to ask the question "what is meant by 'global?'"
Rather like the words "innovative" and "creative" are used interchangeably, "global" and "international" mean whatever the writer chooses them to mean. Sumantra Ghoshal and Christopher Bartlett (see Chapter 8) have very specific definitions of the four terms "multinational," "global," "international," and "transnational." For the sake of convenience we have used these definitions as a starting point. However our quick-fire definition of what is meant by "global" training and development is any international training and development initiative that is launched, designed, and/or delivered from the center. Local initiatives to meet purely local needs – like routine office-skills training – do not count, even if they are undertaken in Hanoi or Asmara rather than Detroit or Birmingham.

Q2: How does "global" training differ from any other kind?

A: In delivery, very little. The key processes of training or organizational needs analysis, design, choice of location, choice of supplier, choice of medium, group work, and post-event appraisal follow similar lines.

Global initiatives tend to vary in three ways. First, by virtue of being linked to growth-based strategy, they are nearly always launched and assessed from the center, even though the task of sustaining the initiative is often devolved to local centers. Given the geographical and logistical dimension, this requires HR practitioners at the top with both visionary and management skills.

Second, the cross-cultural complexities of global management, explored in Chapters 3, 4, and 6, mean that local workforces in developing economies may not respond to basic management concepts – quality management, cross-functional working, project leadership, empowerment, and so on – in the way their counterparts do "at home." This means that the training and/or organizational needs analysis that determines the exact design of the initiative has to be exceptionally rigorous, and undertaken or contributed to by individuals with an insight into the social and economic forces that shape local attitudes and behavior.

Third, as stressed in Chapter 10, events move very quickly in fast-growing or volatile economies. Politics has a direct impact on strategy and local workforce attitudes (as illustrated by the profile of General Electric in Chapter 4), reliable suppliers close or move on, "world events" intervene in a way they do not "at home." This means HR practitioners commissioning or supervising work from a distance need to stay in touch and take nothing on trust or for granted.

Q3: How does "boundaryless" fit in?

A: When Jack Welch of General Electric (GE) developed the term "boundaryless," it was before the dramatic expansion of the company into Central Europe and Asia. He used the word "boundary" to describe internal boundaries as well as geographical ones. Writing in GE's 1994 annual report, he commented: "People seem compelled to build walls between themselves and others that, above all, slows things down."

Of course, the expansion of globalism in the 1990s has added geographical and cultural boundaries to the equation. But so has Internet working and cross-functional working. The rather trite conclusion is to say that while globalism and boundarylessness are closely interlinked, global companies are not always boundaryless and boundaryless organizations are not always global.

Q4: Who invented the mantra "think global, act local?"

A: Many people have laid claim to the phrase, but the originator is generally accepted to be Sweden's Percy Barnevik, the former chairman and chief executive of engineering conglomerate Asea Brown Boveri (ABB). Unfortunately, Barnevik's star faded when he quit executive control of ABB to oversee the Wallenberg dynasty's other investments; and ABB, unlike GE, failed to sustain its performance after the master manager left the scene.

It was left to others to explore how to resolve this difficult strategic equation. In HR terms, the best authority is the University of Michigan's Dave Ulrich. His list of goals is summarized in Chapters 4 and 8.

Q5: How do corporate social responsibilities apply in global markets and what role does training have in supporting them?

A: This is a subject for a whole book. By virtue of their wealth and resources, and the significant impact they have on fragile local economies, global corporations have become the most significant engines of social transformation in the developing world – more powerful than governments, armies, and the church. Yet, thanks largely to nineteenth-century limited liability laws that still define corporate governance, they remain unaccountable to the countries and people they most affect.

In the past decade attempts been made to draw up universally acceptable codes of practice that govern issues like how investment is made and withdrawn; what exemptions (if any) global corporations should enjoy under local tax and employment protection legislation; and how technologies that might benefit local economies should be transferred and sustained. Two of these attempts – by the UN's Carlos Fortin and Canon chairman Ryuzaburo Kaku – are summarized in Chapter 8.

Whether or how corporations should respond is clearly outside the remit of the global HR manager. But an exploration of the issues can and, in our view, should form part of any boardroom education initiative. The ExpressExec guide *Boardroom Education* explores how this can be introduced and managed.

Index

EXPRESSEXEC –
BUSINESS THINKING AT YOUR FINGERTIPS

ExpressExec is a 12-module resource with 10 titles in each module. Combined they form a complete resource of current business practice. Each title enables the reader to quickly understand the key concepts and models driving management thinking today.

Available from:
www.expressexec.com

Customer Service Department
John Wiley & Sons Ltd
Southern Cross Trading Estate
1 Oldlands Way, Bognor Regis
West Sussex, PO22 9SA
Tel: +44(0)1243 843 294
Fax: +44(0)1243 843 303
Email: cs-books@wiley.co.uk